© FAMOLARE ®

Sales Offices
4 West 58th Street
at Fifth Avenue
New York, New York 10019
Phone: 212 - 593-1471

Dear Friends:

The Fashion Makers is a photo
journalistic profile of America's
top fifty fashion designers.
Barbra Walz has spent over two
years photographing these designers
"so that people could see the faces
behind the names." The accompanying
text was written by Bernadine Morris
and profiles each designer's lifestyle.

We at Famolare feel that Barbra and
Bernadine's book is a significant
contribution to the American Fashion
Industry, and take this opportunity
to give a complimentary copy to all
of you who have shared in the development of both Famolare and the
American Fashion Industry as a whole.

Corporate Offices — Ferry Road, P.O. Box 597, Brattleboro, Vermont 05301, Phone: 802 - 254-8741

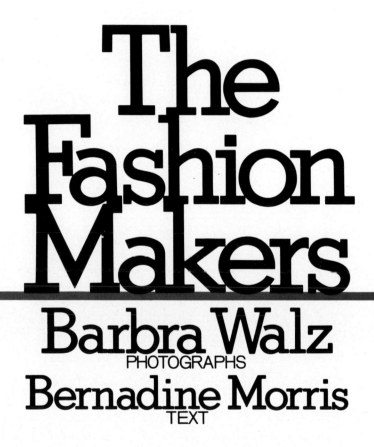

The Fashion Makers

Barbra Walz
PHOTOGRAPHS

Bernadine Morris
TEXT

RANDOM HOUSE   NEW YORK

Photographs Copyright© 1978 by Barbra Walz
Text Copyright© 1978 by Bernardine Morris

All rights reserved under International and Pan-American
Copyright Conventions. Published in the United States by
Random House, Inc., New York, and simultaneously in
Canada by Random House of Canada Limited, Toronto.

*Grateful acknowledgment is made to the following for
permission to reprint previously published material:*
The New York Times: "Profile of Giorgio Sant' Angelo" by
Bernadine Morris, July 7, 1977. Copyright© 1977 by The New
York Times Company.

Library of Congress Cataloging in Publication Data
Walz, Barbra.
  The fashion makers.
  1. Costume designers—United States. I. Morris, Bernadine.
II. Title.
TT507.W218   779′.9′746920922   77-6028
ISBN 0-394-41166-8

Manufactured in the United States of America
98765432

DESIGN BY KEVIN WALZ

For Aunt Louise, with love

Contents

Introduction

by Barbra Walz

As a child I was always interested in fashion. Aunt Louise took me on shopping sprees down Fifth Avenue twice a year from the time I was seven. As a teenager I read *Seventeen* and *Glamour,* bought fabric and patterns and tried to make a new outfit each weekend. When I was not voted "best dressed" at my high school graduation I was devastated. I entered Pratt Institute as a fashion student, but by the second semester I realized it was not for me. I transferred to the photography department and resolved never to get near fashion again.

In 1972, after Pratt, I was drawn back into the fashion industry by a close friend named Joan Grady. Joan wrote a daily fashion newspaper column and asked me if I would take pictures to illustrate her articles. My first assignment was a portrait of a designer named Giorgio Sant' Angelo. Without knowing anything about who he was, I dashed up to his West Fifties studio with my cameras. His red office was alive with photographs, fabrics, models and mementos of his travels from all over the world. Giorgio was a dashing Italian with a fantastic face and I fell in love with him immediately. We talked about fashion, designing, art school and Walt Disney for about

an hour before even beginning to shoot. When I left I knew I wanted to become a part of this industry and its creativity.

Later that year I got a job photographing designers and their collections for another newspaper. My portfolio began to develop as my own impression of the industry and its designers. I shot Blass, de la Renta, Klein and Lauren in their individual environments. I always tried to bring out some part of their personality for the public to see. I found a magic in the designers I photographed. They were devoted artists, creating exciting things each season for their customers. I also became aware that the public was reacting to them on a new level—they had become celebrities. Halston was designing sheets and towels, and so were Calvin and Oscar; Geoffrey was starting a new perfume, and Bill was even designing the interiors of cars. One evening over dinner, Carol Horn told me that a firm had expressed an interest in designer pots and pans and that she was even considering doing them. Designers were in magazines, on the radio and in television commercials, and were making not only clothes but sunglasses, umbrellas, luggage, shoes, jewelry and cosmetics.

Before long I realized that I wanted to show America what these "fashion makers" were like. Sure, each had a press photo for news stories and publicity, but I wanted to cut through all the stereotypes, see how these people worked, where they lived and what they did for fun.

For the next year I lived with and photographed fifty American designers. I shot them with husbands, wives, lovers, dogs, cats and birds; in gardens, country houses, restaurants, department stores, perfume factories, swimming pools, bathtubs, gyms and even dentists' offices. I traveled with them in limousines, planes, helicopters and even on horses. My only hope was to get to know them and capture the essence of their life style with my cameras. Before I photographed anyone, I would talk to them and then together we would formulate how to handle the way they would be presented in the book. I shot from fifteen to thirty roles of film on each designer and, in preparing the book, sifted through more than thirty thousand photographs.

While in California I called Jimmy Galanos. He was busy at work on his new collection and refused to see me. He raved about how he hated photographers and having his picture taken. My persistent phone calls finally made him consent to one photograph of him working at his desk. I tried to relax him by talking about the book and some of my experiences with other designers. Before long we left his office and he felt comfortable enough to have me shoot in his workrooms. Galanos then casually said he wanted to show me his Rolls-Royce. After we finished at the studio he took the afternoon off and we photographed at his home in the Hollywood Hills. In a short time he had gone from being angry at the thought of being photographed to enjoying and making the most of our session. Galanos ended the afternoon by showing me a beautiful collection of portraits he had taken with his own camera some twenty years ago.

I wanted to photograph Stephen Burrows doing something crazy. I imagined him on a roller coaster and discussed the possibility of attempting something like that. He told me he had ridden the Cyclone on Coney Island ten times in a row last summer and would love to try it again. I sat in front of him, firmly secured my camera and photographed through two rides around. After it was all over, I was queasy from sitting backwards and focusing on Stephen; how I managed to get back to the city I'll never understand.

I photographed Bill Blass at his apartment in New York and was not pleased with my results. Bill is a man with a definite self-image. He is constantly being photographed and knows exactly what he wants to project on film. I wanted to break that image. I called him and we arranged for one more try. As I left my house I grabbed about a dozen apples I had just brought back from Vermont. I decided to photograph him eating the apples—and who other than Bill Blass best represents the "big apple"? The apples completely relaxed him, and as he juggled one up I caught one of my favorite images. Since that shooting, Bill has allowed me to photograph him jumping off fences, climbing trees and standing under umbrellas in the rain. He is completely at ease with my camera and I think I have uncovered the real Bill Blass.

One of the designers I was most anxious to meet was Edith Head, a woman I have admired for years. During our first day of shooting at her home in Beverly Hills I noticed a funny little structure behind her garage. She led me into the tiny fireproof cube; hanging in it were hundreds of the original designs worn by Dietrich, Garbo, Crawford, Monroe and Taylor. She carried them out carefully, one by one, so I could see them in the natural light. As Edith stood in front of her garage I photographed her with those famous dresses that had won her so many Oscars.

When it came time to shoot Elsa Peretti I found her busy at work renovating a fifteenth-century village near Barcelona in Spain. I spent five days photographing her in this exquisite rustic environment. On the last day she asked me to photograph her underwater in the pool she had built on the second story of an old ruin. I climbed up a twelve-foot ladder on top of a van and shot Peretti through a sealed window as she swam.

I have had hundreds of experiences and gone through some extraordinary times with these people, and they have given me some amazingly high moments. It is always incredibly exciting to investigate a total stranger on film. I realize that when I decide to photograph someone, somehow it means that I want to know him or her. Something very special takes place when I enter someone's life with my camera—a friendship begins.

11

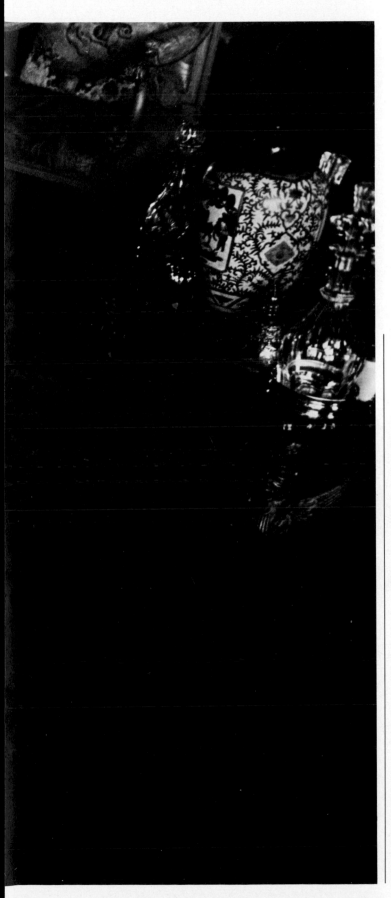

Adolfo

Adolfo just might be the most amiable man in fashion. His customers adore him. They're rich women, known and unknown, from all over the country, wherever Saks Fifth Avenue (his major outlet) has stores. Twice a year for two months at a spell, he travels around the country meeting his fans, many of whom turn up at his salon when they get to New York.

"I just live in Adolfo's clothes," said Harriet Deutsch, a West Coast fan, who simply had to run into his Madison Avenue shop on a visit to New York. "The simple ones are for traveling, the ruffles and feathers are for dressing up," she explained.

Other Californians who feel the same way are Betsy Bloomingdale, Marlo Thomas, Denise Hale and Anne Getty. New York admirers include Jan Chipman, Lauren Peltz, Joanne Cummings and Nan Kempner, who wear his clothes to fashionable parties and Gloria Vanderbilt Cooper, who doesn't go out that much. They're all attractive women who care about how they look and don't worry unduly about prices.

Adolfo learned how to relate to his customers when he began in fashion, designing hats. He worked for Emme, one of the grand milliners, before opening his own business in 1962 with $10,000 he borrowed from Bill Blass. "I repaid it six months later," he recalled. Though his business prospered,

13

Adolfo wasn't content just making hats. He was determined to make clothes too. So when everybody ran off to cocktail parties in the early evening, Adolfo studied dressmaking with an elegant Cuban woman he knew.

Originally, he would make the dresses his models wore when they showed his hats. Then he started making clothes for Gloria Vanderbilt Cooper. "She was my inspiration—we worked out things together," he says. They still do. They also exchange books. Adolfo is a great reader. At times he concentrates on eighteenth-century French authors. Other times he's attracted by the Elizabethans. In between he reads novels. "If I didn't have to work, I would be content to be a scholar," he says.

He was born Adolfo Sardina in Cuba and raised by an aunt, his mother having died in childbirth. His aunt was one of those fashionable Latin women with a fondness for the French couture. Balenciaga was her favorite, but after Chanel reopened her business in the 1950's, she switched over to Chanel.

"She was the most extraordinary woman," Adolfo says, speaking of the French designer. "I met her four times with my aunt, but I was always too shy to talk to her—she always seemed so busy."

His first successes in the fashion field were knitted styles in the manner of Chanel. Later he began impressing women with his extravagantly feminine evening clothes. "Some-

14

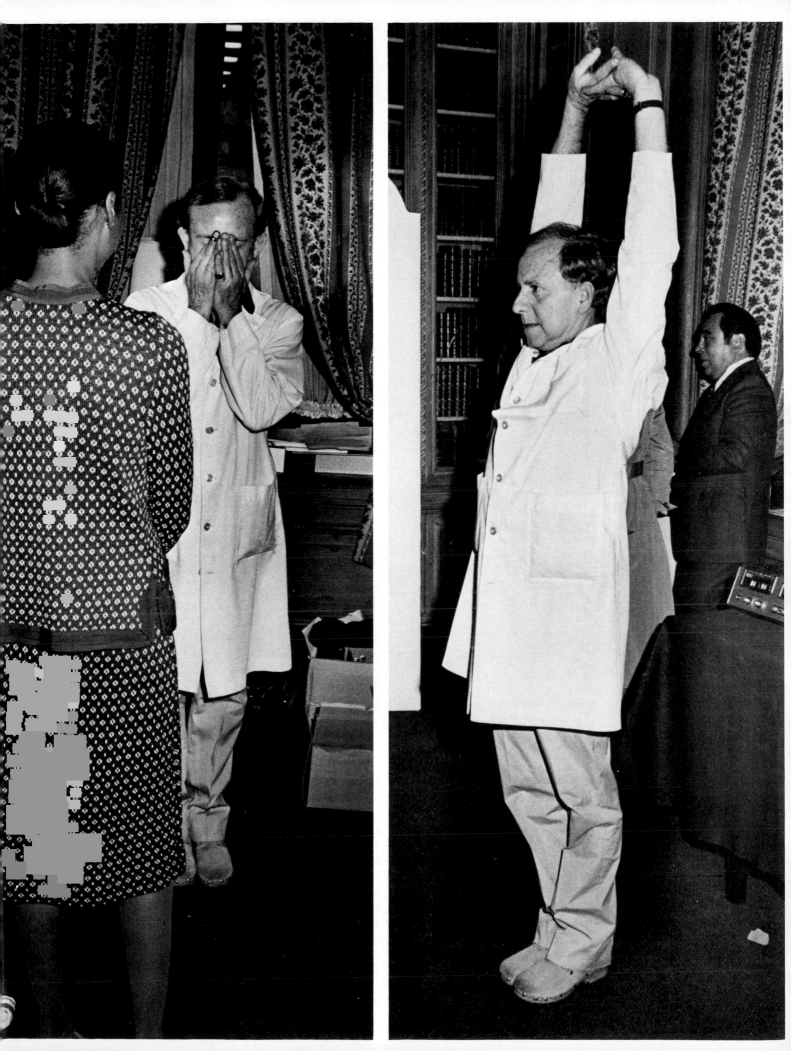

Adri

Adrienne Steckling—she calls herself Adri—is one of those tall, rangy women who consoled themselves when they were teenagers with the thought that they were built like models. At five feet nine and a half inches, she was "just about one foot too tall" during adolescence. She grew up in St. Joseph, Missouri, and at the height of her discomfort, when she was about fifteen, her parents took her to Hot Springs, Arkansas, on a vacation. Going shopping with her mother in that resort town, she fell in love with a designer named Claire McCardell. "Maybe," she says now, "because her clothes were the first things that fit me—she seemed to make clothes for women who were ten feet tall."

Her mother bought her a McCardell dress "even though she thought fifty dollars was pretty excessive for a high school girl." When they got home, they copied the dress many times, and McCardell, one of the great pioneers of sports clothes in this country, became her idol.

There are people in the fashion world who consider Adri the inheritor of McCardell's mantle as the leading exponent of soft, feminine, casual sportswear. Like her idol, Adri designs for herself. She makes clothes she can feel comfortable wearing, clothes that are pretty but relaxed. Often they have an original twist. She likes deep, cuddly cowl collars, full dirndl skirts.

"There's something useful about being a woman designing for women. You can test the style on yourself. You know what you want to wear, and if you are lucky you find other women who agree with you. An ivory tower is out of the question. You don't think of clothes in abstract terms. You have to be realistic. I'd been wearing pants for a number of years—I love them, but I was getting tired of them—so I decided I would wear culottes. That gave me the convenience of pants but the feeling of a skirt. It turned out that appealed to other women too. I just didn't decide 'Let there be culottes.'"

She believes that "designing is perfecting an idea" and that a designer's collection

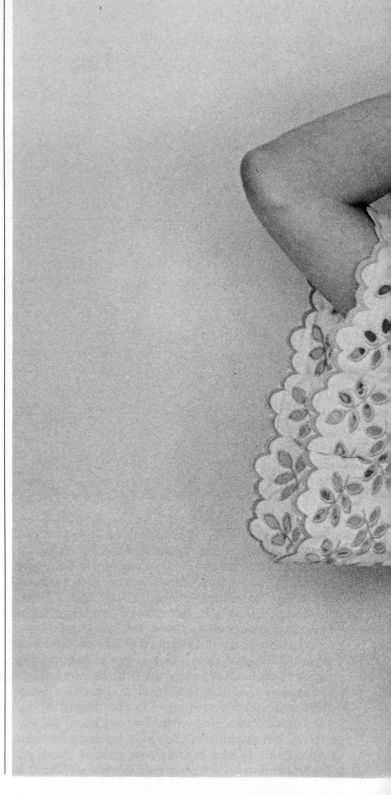

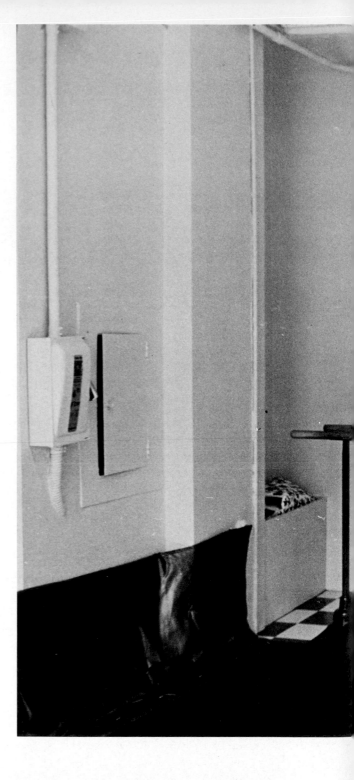

Adri with Frank Olive at Metropolitan Museum opening.

should have a continuity from one season to another.

"The ideal is finding a look that adapts to changes and can be updated constantly, like Chanel's or McCardell's. Something that's identifiable. I didn't do that. I went all over the lot in the beginning, and I'm sorry now."

She had studied retailing and design at Washington University in St. Louis and won a place on *Mademoiselle* magazine's college board. She transferred to Parsons School of Design and eventually landed a job doing serious, expensive sports clothes at B.H.

Wragge. When she started her own business in 1966, "I intentionally went the opposite route—I did crazy things because I had to prove to the world I had my own personality."

Among the crazy things were accordion-pleated dresses that hung straight from the neckline and were worked into odd geometric shapes. The well-known designer Mila Schoen in Milan did the same thing at about the same time, which brought Adri's new company a certain amount of notoriety. She also made clear plastic raincoats that related to the designs of the dress underneath them. If both were striped diagonally, a plaid

effect was formed when the raincoat was worn over the dress.

The crazy things of the 1960's are behind her now. She is interested in clothes that are easy to care for "because I have no patience with dry cleaners any more." She thinks clothes should fit a variety of figures "because stores simply don't have the facilities to cope with extensive alterations." Properly designed, with the assistance of drawstrings, wrapped effects and carefully thought out gathers, clothes in three sizes, marked Petite, Small and Medium, should fit everyone from size four to size fourteen.

Her collection of leisure clothes, or what she prefers to call leisure sportswear, for Royal Robes was a big success, though they're not only for women of leisure. For the most part, they're soft jersey pieces that are comfortable enough to be worn around the house, but they can also be worn out to lunch or for dancing. The multiple function is part of today. "Americans are reorganizing their lives," she says. "We're all interested in simplified living."

Adri has started a new venture—designing sportswear for Jerry Silverman. The kind of soft clothes she's always specialized in is in vogue, and this may be the beginning of a new era for Adri.

Gil Aimbez

"Someday, I would like to dress an entire family—from the very young to the very old." It's an offbeat idea, but Gil Aimbez is an offbeat designer. His clothes for Genre include voluminous shapes and skinny ones. He does fluffy peasant clothes and sleek jersey styles. His clothes are in the sportswear category, but they're not conventional sportswear. He doesn't make blazers. Everything is soft and fluid and the prices are modest.

A typical Aimbez customer is a girl in her late teens or early twenties who, a few years back, tie-dyed her T-shirts and embroidered her blue jeans. Now she's broadened her range, but she doesn't want to look like the women in the garden club. She understands innovation and she wants to be comfortable.

In Aimbez's first season at Genre, the company booked one and a half million dollars' worth of business. He was specializing in cotton-gauze styles, just what the avant-garde customer was wearing. "I didn't want to do run-of-the-mill clothes. What this garment center doesn't need is another manufacturer making basics."

So Aimbez constantly varies his style, offering clothes for different moods, sometimes doing romantic styles, sometimes austere ones. Happily, he can get the effects he wants because, unlike some designers, he is a good technician, skilled at cutting, pattern making, draping and grading.

Aimbez was born in Los Angeles, and his ancestry is Japanese, Filipino and Mexican. The ninth in a family of thirteen children, he says, "I didn't want to wear hand-me-downs, so I had to design my way out."

He takes clothes seriously. "If people compliment you on what you wear, it puts you in a good frame of mind, and you pass this good feeling on to everyone you meet that day."

A collector of books and antiques, he says he is greatly influenced by the past. "I block out new buildings; when I was in Japan, I blocked out everyone who wasn't in a kimono. I guess you would call me a romantic."

With his emphasis on ease and comfort, he's an eminently contemporary designer. "I'm not old enough to remember the past and I'm young enough to relate to the present," he says.

Besides being relaxed, clothes are getting more sophisticated, he believes. The easy, comfortable shapes are far more interesting than stiff, structured ones. They are also applicable to women of all ages. "I never wanted to dress ten percent of the public," he says. "I want the mothers—and the daughters too. Some years ago, that wouldn't have been practical. Today it is."

John Anthony

John Anthony believes clothes should be modern. That means (1) they're in soft, supple shapes that move with the body; (2) they're in interchangeable parts which can be switched around to accommodate all occasions; and (3) they're in muted colors which never stare out at you.

"It's the only intelligent way to approach fashion today," he observes. "If a woman wants to travel with twenty-five pieces of Vuitton, that's her business. But the modern woman travels with one suitcase. From eight or ten pieces of clothing—skirts, shirts, sweaters, jackets and pants—she can pull together fifteen or sixteen looks. That's enough to take her through a two-week trip with plenty of changes."

Anthony thinks that coats have to be constructed so they can be thrown in the hatch of an airplane. That's one reason why his are always soft, the kind that can be rolled up with no danger of wrinkling. And with his muted-color palette, one coat can easily go with everything else in his collection.

He obviously doesn't believe in excess baggage; one pair of shoes for day and another for evening are all a woman need take with her when she is traveling. Even when she stays home, Anthony sees no need for endless closets full of clothes. Having just a few things that work for you is what he recommends.

His collections reflect his orderly thinking. While most designers show in the neighborhood of a hundred designs, his collections contain half that number. "If I can't present my story in thirty minutes, I shouldn't be doing what I'm doing."

In his own life he is even more economical. He owns a gray suit, a navy blue suit and a

beige suit. He has a brown coat and a black one, a dinner jacket, six shirts and six pairs of pants. His brown coat is six years old and has never been cleaned. Dry cleaners mutilate clothes, he believes. He has his steamed and pressed regularly and spot-cleaned if necessary. He insists that his sweaters be hand-washed.

"People don't have to spend a king's ransom on clothes, they just have to be sensible about them," he insists. His own clothes are made to measure because he is small in stature and slight. They're in the best fabrics he can find, and so is the quality of workmanship. That's why they last so long and ultimately prove economical.

He thinks about his collections long before he puts hand to fabric. For a typical winter collection he will decide to show perhaps six colors. By the time he starts working he may have eliminated one of them. When he opened his first collection under his own name in 1971, he showed mostly black clothes, with a smattering of navy, white and red.

"A chic woman doesn't wear fuchsia or turquoise," he said then. He still feels that way about shock colors, but his favorite colors now are in the range of off-white to brown. He calls them fawn, cinnamon, peanut and so on. He's also fond of pale gray.

Having selected his colors, he will have fabrics such as chiffon, jersey, satin and wool dyed in each shad. Each color will then represent a mini collection in itself, and a woman could pick everything in the same shade. Or if she prefers more variety, she could choose different shades and be assured that they would each work with the others. That is what he considers the designer's job: to make things easier for the customer.

28

John cavorts with model Pat Cleveland on the West Side Highway.

His fashion philosophy did not emerge full blown; it evolved slowly. His first collection featured mannish tailoring: his suits were broad-shouldered, pin-striped or in herring-bone wools. "Very Marlene Dietrich," observers noted. But underneath the suits, a soft blouse appeared. And his first dresses were tucked, pleated or smocked, details that were to stay with him.

In a subsequent collection he emphasized red fox on almost everything, most often blending with apricot or cinnamon wools. Later he tried his hand at playclothes, introducing bikinis, terry-cloth wraps and off-the-shoulder tops for the summer of 1975. The following fall his jumpsuit was the big success, but it was the spring collection in 1976 that saw the emergence of his special style. "I've been trying to do it for five years and I've finally found the way," he exclaimed at the time. The way was separates in fabrics so soft they seemed liquid, so light the mannequins seemed unburdened by the fabric that swept around them. There were plenty of tucks, pleats and ties, and the colors were soft and melting.

He enunciated his aim when he showed his next collection: "I want my clothes to be

modern. The way I do this is by using the most luxurious fabrics in the simplest shapes." This is the path he has been pursuing ever since. It has brought him calls from the White House to do clothes for Presidents' wives (Mrs. Ford and Mrs. Carter), from a former President's wife (Mrs. Onassis) and from entertainers such as Audrey Meadows and Lena Horne. But best of all, it has brought him a loyal following of women who feel the way he does about clothes and are happy that he has done the organizing for them.

John Anthony lives in a brownstone on Manhattan's East Side with a fireplace in every room. He and his wife, Molly—they were recently separated—used to ski every winter in Vermont. They have a teenage son, Marc.

The designer was born Gianantonio Iorio in Queens, where his father was a metalworker. A graduate of the High School of Industrial Art and the Fashion Institute of Technology, he designed for Devonbrook, Adolph Zelinka and other coat and suit houses before starting his own company in 1971.

"I've been twenty years in the business, but I learned the most in the last seven, when I was on my own," he says. "The true art of design is to mingle function and purpose."

Scott Barrie

Scott Barrie's clothes are sexy, sometimes outrageous. His best efforts are for evening, when women are more likely to want to be noticed than they are during the day. And Barrie's evening dresses are not designed for wallflowers. He slits them up the sides, which is necessary because they're so skinny that without slits the wearer wouldn't be able to walk. He sprinkles them with brilliants. He makes cape-like tops that are cut in a full circle, forming a half-moon when the arms are extended. His forte is jersey, and jersey slithers, even if it's cut full, with smocking, as he likes to do. Those who notice such things will spot his marvelously inventive cuts, with seams in unexpected places or with no seams at all.

His dresses are worn by Naomi Sims, the startlingly beautiful black model who orders them in white, and by Lee Traub, the wife of the president of Bloomingdale's and a woman who has her choice of the best clothes in the world.

All the women in his family sewed, but none of them encouraged him to be a designer. "My mother told me, 'It's hard to break into that field,'" he says. "'Blacks don't make it there." He pauses, grins, and adds triumphantly, "We changed all that." "We" means himself, Jon Haggins, Willi Smith, Stephen Burrows—the black designers who, along with the vibrant black models, crashed Seventh Avenue during the glory days of the 1960's. They brought with them a brashness, a vitality and a creative energy that stimulated the world of fashion. On the runways, the models danced, teased and strutted

Scott checks models before his fashion show.

instead of gliding along disdainfully with their eyes fixed on the middle distance. The clothes they wore were colorful, original, and sometimes outlandish. Collectively they cracked the color barrier and brought a fresh style along with them. "We helped each other," recalls Mr. Barrie. "We sent each other customers."

What was the reaction to his being black? "There's always someone who doesn't like the idea," he acknowledged. "But I was lucky to run into people who didn't care—in fact, who wanted to help me." It was the time of freedom rides and civil rights rallies when he began. "It's probably harder today for a black designer," he went on. "You really have to be good. You can't get by on being black. It may be simpler to get in the door, but you are in competition with everyone else who is there, not just the other blacks."

He thinks of himself as a middle-of-the-road designer. "I'm not as crazy as Zandra Rhodes, but I'm a little more crazy than Kasper," he says.

When he left Philadelphia, where he was born and where he studied at the Philadelphia Museum College of Art, he came to New York and started making clothes for the

boutiques. He had a sewing machine and a makeshift cutting table in his apartment. He always kept a piece of paper or a pad handy so he could sketch ideas as they came to him.

He had the idea for a group of jersey dresses—"neat, bare and short or long"—which he sold to Bendel's. Then Bloomingdale's came along.

"When you're in Bendel's and Bloomingdale's, the rest of the country comes around," he says. He no longer had to work in his apartment. He kept renting space for his workroom—and outgrowing it. In 1972, ten years after he arrived in New York, he moved to 530 Seventh Avenue, one of the prestige buildings in the garment district. He had arrived.

He has goals. He would like to sell his clothes in Europe the way clothes from France and Italy are sold here. He would like to have a perfume with his name on it. Meanwhile he has the responsibility of running his business. He says that sometimes when a messenger comes into his office to deliver a package, he feels envious of him because he doesn't have anything else on his mind but getting that package there. But the mood passes. He enjoys being Scott Barrie, fashion designer. "I love what I'm doing. I make a decent living. I know I'm a lucky man."

Geoffrey Beene

Geoffrey Beene is fascinated by George Orwell, especially *1984*. He rereads it from time to time and finds it an excellent guide to contemporary life. As a designer, he is not only concerned with dressing people for today; he is also thinking about tomorrow.

In many innovative ways, Mr. Beene is the most prestigious designer in the United States today. And what pleases him exceedingly is the fact that he is being recognized as a force beyond national borders.

He has shown his collection in Australia. In 1976 he opened an office in Milan where he not only presents his clothes but sells them to stores in Common Market countries and in Japan and South Africa.

"We sell to every major country in the world," he says. "Germany is first, then Japan, England and Italy." France has been the slowest to accept Beene clothes, but he expects it to buy them soon.

Beene is no newcomer to the world of fashion. He landed on Seventh Avenue in the 1950's, learned his craft painstakingly, and was one of the first designers to set up their own business in 1963. In 1968 he made the dress Lynda Bird Johnson wore to her White House wedding. He was a traditionalist, known for his high-waisted Empire dresses with braid-edged architectural lines that flattered everyone.

Like other prestigious Seventh Avenue designers, he made not only an expensive collection but several less expensive, more casual ones to reach a wider group of people.

In the early 1970's, with the fashion business in dire straits and the country in an economic crisis, he began to question what he was doing. "I began rethinking the question of clothes and their relation to how people lived, how comfortable they felt, how they fit into the pace of modern living. I began to conceptualize what I was doing. I spent some time in museums, looking back on the clothes people wore for five hundred years to see what I could adapt for today. I considered giving up the more expensive clothes, but I decided against it. I knew there would always be people who wanted quality, there would always be people who could afford it. But I decided I would aim at the younger generation, who didn't want the stiff kind of constructed clothes other people and I had been making."

But more important, he decided to redesign his Beene Bag collection along younger, sportier lines. It would be relatively inexpensive—even today he doesn't pay more than five dollars a yard for fabric—and it would be geared to the pace of contemporary living. "It was actually romanticized sportswear," he recalls. "It consisted of soft things that could be rolled up and put in a tote bag—or could be worn with a more tailored jacket. I figured if I put a certain amount of taste and style in cheaper clothes they couldn't miss." He found inexpensive fabrics like mattress ticking and used them in styles that were looser and softer than the ones generally being shown.

Beene Bag was an instant success. "The slightest acceptance was all the incentive I needed to go on with the idea," he recalls. He discovered there was no need to be apologetic about his cheaper clothes. Ideas from the less expensive line were adapted to his more expensive clothes and vice versa. Everything became looser, more flowing.

"Anything static just doesn't work for modern living," he says. "If a woman dashes about, her clothes should move with her or else they become a hindrance, they do not serve a purpose. The nature of fashion is changing, and we have to find a new

Geoffrey in his garden on Fire Island.

terminology to describe it. Fashion is no longer defined as a pretty dress. The important thing is how the dress works. I see my role as a designer as trying to make people's lives easier."

Beene is now concerned with translating some of this ease into men's clothes. Men haven't known the comfort women have been learning to expect in their clothes. In his Beene Bag for men, he is trying to loosen up the fit of men's clothes. The styles are aimed at those people who have outgrown blue jeans, have become affluent but are not yet ready to accept establishment clothes. "It won't be easy, but it will be fun," he says.

The Beene Bag women's collections are "possibly the easiest things I have ever done," he says. "Once I got the concept, the things just began to happen. Everything crystallized in my mind."

Now he is wondering about the future, the Orwellian future. He is fascinated by the possibilities of synthetic fabrics. He is concerned with new ways of constructing and finishing clothes.

"Fashion is my way of contributing to other human beings," he says. "It is my way of communicating with people, of making something better in their lives. And the most gratifying thing is that it doesn't work just in this country—it's working all over the world."

Geoffrey Beene is a quiet, amiable man who enjoys good talk and good food. He tries out new restaurants for their cuisine, not their clientele. He doesn't care to be seen wherever it is chic to be seen. His life is private, his manner gracious.

His speech still has overtones of his Southern background—he was born and brought up in Haynesville, Louisiana. He studied medicine at Tulane, in New Orleans, before heading for Paris, where he became an art student at the Académie Julian ("where Toulouse Lautrec went to school"), California and, eventually, New York. After eight years at Harmay, a Seventh Avenue dress house, and a few with Teal Traina, who put his name on the label and started his climb to success, Beene opened his own business in 1964. Now his influence transcends New York: a Southern gentleman has become a gentleman of the world.

Bill Blass

Nancy Kissinger comes to his fashion shows on Seventh Avenue. So do Mary Beame, Happy Rockefeller and a host of other women whose names are less well known but whose social credentials are impeccable.

He is Bill Blass, as celebrated for his life style as for the clothes he designs. His name also sells automobiles, men's toiletries and sheets. An urbane gentleman with landed-gentry manners, he was born in Indiana. Seventh Avenue's most celebrated Hoosier, he has helped raise the status and the standing of what used to be known as the rag business. Thanks to the Blass efforts, ready-to-wear gained stature. The fashion designer became a socially desirable guest or escort.

Until he began inviting women he met at dinner parties and weekends in Southampton to his seasonal openings, it was not usual to find anyone but store buyers, an occasional upper-echelon retail executive and fashion reporters at ready-to-wear showings. In Paris, it was different, of course. Those were made-to-order collections. The women came to the showings to see what they could buy for themselves. But Seventh Avenue—that was something else. Nobody went there except the buyers who would select the styles to be presented in their stores' posh salons—the manufacturing center was déclassé.

"When I started working, the designer was kept in the back," Mr. Blass recalls. "We never emerged to meet the buyers and the press. As soon as we finished a collection, we were encouraged to take a month off. That's so the clothes could be 'modified' or 'adapted' and we wouldn't be around to complain."

At that time—the late 1940's and the early

Bill at his country house in Connecticut, with assistant Tom Fallon.

1950's—the designer generally worked for a manufacturer whose name was on the door and on the label too. The woman who bought the clothes was aware of the manufacturer—in Blass's case, Maurice Rentner—rather than the designer, who was as anonymous as the seamstress who sewed the garment.

Blass changed that too. First, he became a partner. Eventually he bought out his associates and the business was his. His name appeared on the door. He determined what styles would be shown. Nobody changed them behind his back.

This went on simultaneously with his appearance as a man about town. Tall. Good-looking. Suntanned skin. Solid build, which he keeps on the trim side with exercise and regular visits to the Golden Door health spa. He says today that he began to be asked out "as an extra man who had two legs and a dinner jacket." He was also witty and charming, and he had a great desire to see how the rich lived. It was necessary, he felt, because he made clothes for them.

When he got his first job on Seventh Avenue as a sketcher, after serving for three years in the U.S. Army during World War II, he would save his money so he could go "uptown to the grand places" for lunch. When he hired Missy Weston, a socially prominent girl, as his model, the two went to a lot of parties together. He met people from publishing, politics and the arts.

Seeing how these people lived helped him decide what kind of clothes he would make for them. He had two strong areas: casual or tailored styles for day, glamorous styles for evening. Unlike many designers, he became as adept at doing ruffles as he was at making suits.

Always interested in clothes for himself—even when he was growing up in Fort Wayne, Indiana—he decided to do a men's collection in the 1960's. It was rather English in feeling, with lots of good tweeds and solid tailoring. "The lady who gave me the big boost," he says, "was Mildred Custin, who was president of Bonwit Teller—she decided

Nancy Kissinger and her dog at a fitting for her spring wardrobe.

to devote a shop to the things.'' Other women admired the men's shirts and sweaters he did and asked why he didn't design that sort of thing for them. Thus Blassport, the sportswear division, was born.

This led to a lot of other design activities in diverse fields. He was one of the first designers to do sheets. Like many other Americans, he's always been fascinated by cars. Along with Hubert de Givenchy, the French couturier, and Emilio Pucci, the Italian, he worked on the interiors of Lincoln Continental's Mark IV and Mark V.

Blass lives in a penthouse surrounded by a terrace overlooking the East River. He has bought a house in Connecticut on twenty-two acres, where he hopes to spend the next couple of years fixing it up and working on the gardens.

He has cut down on his traveling and his socializing. He tries to limit his nights out to three times a week. He says, ''When you spend so much time with people, as a designer must, by the nature of his job, you develop a need for solitude. Anyone who thinks a designer works in an ivory tower is mad. It's a people-oriented profession. I've always enjoyed being with people. I've never had

trouble meeting them or getting along with them. It was a necessity to me as a designer. You have to understand people to make clothes for them because the clothes don't exist in the abstract. But much as I love them, there are times when I feel I have to get away and be by myself. On weekends now, I hardly ever socialize. I go to the country and I never go out."

The designer has moved far from the back room where he was once hidden. "In the 1970's," he says, "the designer became a brand name. His name on the product gave it validity. This helps establish design standards and, on the whole, is a good thing, pro-viding it is not abused."

He tries to ensure that anything with his name on it is designed by him or by an assistant under his supervision. The development pleases him, because it is a sign that the influence of the fashion designer is no longer limited to dresses. Seventh Avenue not only has become socially acceptable but is setting standards for patterns for life styles in other areas besides clothes. Its influence is all-pervasive.

One of his newest projects is designing furs for Maximilian. The label will read "Maximilian for Bill Blass." He's rather pleased about that too.

47

Stephen Burrows

In the annals of fashion Stephen Burrows will go down as a creator. He burst on the scene toward the end of the 1960's and was widely acclaimed as the most inventive and imaginative of designers in a widely innovative period. He mixed up colors with an artist's eye, especially in his pieced or patchwork jerseys that established his first claim to fame. Later came fluttery chiffon dresses, delicate and charming. His clothes were praised as somehow expressing the black experience—not the sober side, but the innate gaiety, exuberance and joy in dressing up.

Of course, his clothes crossed color lines and were appreciated by a white audience as well. But he was recognized as a black designer, and this helped pave the way for other blacks in the fashion field. Black models as well as black designers gave another dimension to the "black is beautiful" philosophy.

Burrows made his first impact in a boutique called "O," which, in addition to his clothes, also sold art objects. Then he moved to Henri Bendel's in New York, where he became part of Bendel's Studio, the store's manufacturing division, which sold his clothes to other stores throughout the country.

His reputation grew. Then, in 1973, he made a misstep. He moved over to Seventh Avenue. He recalls: "I wanted everyone to wear my things. Halston said it was simple. I just had to make the dress, then they would produce it and send it all over America. I found it didn't work that way. I didn't want to make dresses that people could throw in their washing machine. I wanted to work in real fabrics, not in materials that had to be used so you could get the style out at a price. Even if the fabric is synthetic, it should feel like something natural. It shouldn't feel like air in the hand."

His story has a happy ending. He went

51

back to Bendel's top floor after three years and worked with Pat Tennant, who had guided him in his earlier career in the store. His first collection, in April 1977, brought him back to the top in one giant step. About sixty stores clamored for the collection, but most important, the success made him feel comfortable.

"I am supported," he says. "I can do what I want." This is necessary to the artist's temperament, and Burrows functions as an artist. First, he draws the clothes—not a crude working sketch, but a glamorized view of what he wants the style to look like. Then he proceeds to work it out in fabric. "The fabric is the medium, the body is the canvas," he explains. "Everyone says clothes are not an art. I say, 'Why not?' They should be."

He studied art in high school in Newark, where he was born, and went to art school for a year in Philadelphia before signing up with the Fashion Institute of Technology in New York.

He had toyed with the idea of becoming a fashion illustrator until he learned that illustrators didn't decide what to make—they drew other people's designs. Then he thought about designing and went to F.I.T. to learn basic techniques. During a work-project period, he designed blouses and after he finished school he was asked to return. "They let me do what I liked, and then they

following page, Stephen and Bethann Hardison on the Cyclone at Coney Island.

would change them," he said. Soon came the "O" boutique and his career had begun.

Today Stephen Burrows knows who he is and what he wants to do. Fashion, he says, is creating your own style. This goes for the wearer of clothes as well as the maker of them: "Fashion is a personal thing—it's finding clothes that suit your personality and putting them together to suit your style."

In finding his own expression, he has been intrigued by sewing-machine techniques. When he was a child, his grandmother, who was a sample hand, taught him to sew. "I was fascinated by the zigzag stitch on her machine," he recalls. "I put it on everything." Later, when he was making jersey dresses he hated to put a hem on them because it weighed down the dress. He used the zigzag stitch at the bottom instead of a hem to keep the ends from raveling. It gave a fluted effect which someone called the lettuce edge. It became one of his signatures and was widely copied.

"We have to have new techniques to carry out new ideas," he says. "We have to push to the unknown. Everything's starting to look alike. When fashion changes, the technology must change. Otherwise everything gets very boring."

53

Albert Capraro

Albert Capraro remembers the moment as if it were preserved in amber. He had been in business just six months, almost to the day. The phone rang on a Monday morning, and the voice said, "This is the White House calling." At first, he thought it was a joke. But the caller identified herself as Nancy Howe, Betty Ford's secretary, and explained that the President's wife had seen some of Capraro's styles in the Washington *Star* the day before and would like him to design some clothes in fabrics President Ford had brought back from the Orient.

"I had seen the article by Eleni Epstein, so I became convinced the call was legitimate," Capraro recalled a few years later. "The next shock was when Mrs. Howe told me I should come to the White House as soon as possible. I get speechless now when I think of it."

Two days later, the White House limousine met him at the airport and brought him to the

First Lady. He remembers: "She was so erect and attractive. She was wearing a sea-green lounging robe and she came into the room with her hand outstretched and said, 'Mr. Capraro, I want to thank you for coming here to see me.' I told her how happy I was and how proud she had made my parents."

The designer eventually made five dresses for her in the Oriental brocades which she wore for state occasions. But he also brought with him his spring collection, from which she chose a dozen styles.

His business was prospering, but the encounter with Betty Ford and the resulting publicity made it spurt ahead. "We had

hoped to do two million dollars the first year—we hit six million," he said. "Everyone wanted to see what the First Lady bought."

The designer didn't rest on his laurels. He continued experimenting with new shapes, developing his interest in softer fabrics and constructions, making clothes simpler as he saw lives grow more complicated.

In addition to dressing Mrs. Ford, he also began to make clothes for her daughter Susan, who was seventeen when he first met her. His two most famous customers helped shape his collections, with which he tried to encompass the needs of a girl in her late teens and a woman in her fifties. Sometimes

Albert brings his clothes to Betty Ford at Vail, Colorado.

the distinctions were blurred: "Once I showed Mrs. Ford a suit—it had a hunting jacket with suede elbow patches, a pleated kilt and a checked shirt—and she said it was for Susan. I asked her to try it on because I thought it would be good on her, sporty but modern, and she did. Later I kept seeing pictures of her in it. She wore it all over during the last campaign."

From Mrs. Ford, Capraro learned some of the complexities of a modern woman's life: "She was constantly on and off planes, she was always meeting people, she had to have clothes that felt good and once she put them on she could forget about them. As other women left their homes to take jobs, they developed some of the same needs."

Capraro feels capable of solving these needs thanks to the push he had in dealing with the First Lady's. Designing, he believes, is a growing process. His began at the Parsons School of Design, after which he worked for Oscar de la Renta for eight years, developing the boutique collection. It accelerated in his own business when he was thrust into the public eye. His current credo is, "Clothes should not be cumbersome and complicated fashion must work."

Aldo Cipullo

Aldo Cipullo was a jewelry designer at Cartier's, a store known for its elaborate and ornate styles, when he made a simple gold circlet bracelet. Etched on the surface were circles bisected by a line symbolizing the head of a screw. The gold circle was fastened with a screw and a vermeil screwdriver was provided for the purpose. The year was 1969, the time of flower children and the slogan "Make love, not war." He called his design the love bracelet and suggested that couples buy two which they would exchange, like rings. They would each close the other's circle with the screwdriver and never take off their bracelets. The romantic idea caught on. "It became my annuity," says Cipullo, who has since left Cartier. "I receive a royalty check every month."

The bracelet marked a turning point in Cipullo's life. He began using mundane things like nails, knots and dollar signs—the everyday equipment of modern living—as the themes for his designs. He even did a collection of earrings and cuff links based on the myriad shapes of pasta. As it happens, cooking is his passion. "My therapy is the kitchen," he says. Cipullo is Italian—he came to the United States in 1959 from Rome, where his father is a jeweler—and pasta is one of his specialties.

The same year he made the love bracelet Cipullo looked around his apartment on Central Park South (near the New York Athletic Club, where he swims every morning) and decided it no longer satisfied him. The eighteenth-century Italian furniture, the gold-leaf picture frames, the elaborate draperies were mementos of the past. I didn't come to this country to surround myself with yesterday, I have to live for today, he thought. Along with removing the draperies and the antiques, he cleared his mind of the baroque way of thinking.

He had worked for David Webb and for Tiffany's before he joined Cartier's. In all three places, precious metals and gems were combined ornately to look rich and sumptuous. He decided that they all looked like museum pieces; he would work in a modern genre. "To repeat the past is an easy way to get out of thinking, it's an escape. The important thing is to reflect the present," he says.

Now, with his own design studio, he has extended his range from jewelry to textiles. He makes place mats, silverware, china, stationery and leather goods. Nails, screws and ropes continue as design elements. But jewelry remains his flagship. He does belt buckles and money clips for men as well as cuff links and rings. The same motif—the dollar sign, for instance—can be used in all of them. "It's the greatest graphic in the world," he says, "besides being a conversation piece."

Putting the right pair of earrings on a woman is a challenge, "like an artist choosing the right stroke of paint." He mixes black onyx with turquoise, crystal with topaz for offbeat effects. But he has no objection to diamonds. He has a trick of placing diamonds on a gold base so they can be seen from the front as well as the side of the face. No use wasting diamonds. Also, placed close to the face, diamonds take the tiredness out of it, he believes.

"Jewelry should be part of the body," he insists. "It should not stick out from it, but it should be a part of it. It should enhance the person wearing it." He does not see it as an ostentatious display.

Lilly Daché

You wouldn't know it today. She's eighty years old, "give or take a year," and her skin is smooth, her eyes sparkling, her voice throaty and her manner flirtatious. Always near at hand is her husband, who, after more than forty years of marriage, still obviously adores her.

But Lilly Daché, born in France, was an ugly child. Her mother told her she was homely and constantly compared her with her sister. Her sister's hair was curly, Lilly's was stringy. Left-handed, she was forced to write with her right hand. As a consequence, she stuttered and her voice sounded hoarse. She would take red paper flowers and spit on them so the color would come off and rub them on her cheeks. She ran her fingers over lumps of coal and then around her eyes to make them glow. Her mother despaired of ever marrying her off, so at the age of sixteen she was sent to live with an uncle in Atlantic City. "All I wanted was to be pretty, to please people, to be liked," she recalls. "I wanted people to say I was cute."

Later, she would please many people, she would help hundreds of women look not only cute but glamorous. She would become one of the top milliners in New York at a time when hats were considered even more important than dresses. These days, when she is retired and lives part of the year in Delray Beach, Florida, women frequently come up to her and say, "Do you remember me? You made my wedding hat," or "I'll never forget the turban you made for me—I met my husband when I wore it."

Atlantic City didn't appeal to her much and she moved on to Philadelphia. That didn't prove much more exciting, and one day she took the train to New York. Starry-eyed as she left Pennsylvania Station and saw cars flying by in all directions, heard an elevated train rumbling overhead and saw the crowds of people in the streets, she decided, This is life—I know I am in America.

A mile or so up Broadway there was a concentration of smart dress stores and millinery shops. One had a sign saying "Milliner wanted." She went in and got the job, for twenty-five dollars a week. That was the beginning.

Later, she and another girl working in the

Lilly with husband Jean Desprès at home in Delray Beach, Florida.

following page, Lilly at her home in Meudon, France.

shop bought it from the owner. She remembers the first hat she made as her own boss. From scraps of blue velvet that were lying around she put together a turban of four different shades of blue—"We used up all the scraps." A woman bought it for $12.50.

Her clientele grew. "I made all the hats on the head," she recalls, "I would talk to the woman. I would ask her where she planned to wear the hat, what kind of dress she would wear it with. I would find out her likes and dislikes. If she thought her nose was too long, I would pull down the brim so you couldn't see the nose so much. I made everything with love, affection and excitement, with all my heart. I wanted to make people happy."

Soon her shop grew too crowded and she moved a few blocks north to a larger place on 82nd Street. At one time she had two shops. In 1930 she made the big move to the East Side. Eventually she bought two buildings at 78 East 56th Street and remodeled them to her taste. She lived and worked there for thirty-seven years until her retirement.

The film studios sent their starlets to her to be photographed in her hats. Many Hollywood personalities became her fans. She particularly admired Sonja Henie, Audrey Hepburn, Carole Lombard and Marlene Dietrich. Her last customer was Loretta

Young, who came in the salon not knowing she had retired. Lilly's husband, Jean Desprès, who had been with Coty for fifty years, rising from stock boy to executive vice-president, was retiring and she decided to close her business. "I thought I could buy some hats," said the actress. The milliner showed her what was left and the glamorous customer cleaned out the place. She bought thirty hats.

That was in 1968. Recently Lilly and her husband sold the house in Pound Ridge, Connecticut, they had owned for forty-four years along with the two hundred acres that went with it. They have a house outside Paris and an apartment high in a building on 57th Street from which they can see the Statue of Liberty to the south and look north past Central Park to the George Washington Bridge. They can even pick out buildings on the West Side where her "enchanted life" started.

Not that she spends much time looking backward. For the last ten years she has not had a hat on her head. She prefers to wear a wig: "It makes life simpler."

Perry Ellis

Perry Ellis is likely to be one of the names in fashion to be reckoned with in the 1980's. In its first year, his company, Portfolio, has launched a new look within the much worked sportswear area. It's relaxed to the point where its detractors say it's unkempt. His mannequins look as if they just fell out of bed.

"Sexy," say his supporters. "Casual," explains Ellis himself. His clothes represent this attitude toward life today, which he feels is more at ease, more relaxed than before.

"The slouch look" is the way he describes his designs, and it has caught on. That means trousers meant to be worn loose and baggy, jackets that look a size or two too large, ample shirts and sweaters worn over T-shirts. The T-shirts, which men have known about for a long time, are the first of his many layers. He likes them for many reasons, including the practical one that they add warmth in winter, feel cool in the summer and are pleasant next to the skin. The aesthetic reason is that they provide a bit of color next to the face.

Part of the Ellis look involves wearing two pairs of socks—one baggy—with a khaki

shirt and two pastel petticoats.

He didn't arrive at his easy, relaxed look overnight. In fact, he didn't think of designing clothes very early in his life. "I grew up in the 1950's, when it was difficult for a male to consider designing women's clothes," he says.

So instead he studied for a master's degree in retailing at New York University, then became a buyer of sportswear for Miller & Rhoads, the store in Richmond, Virginia. He was so successful that John Meyer of Norwich asked him to join the company as a stylist. It wasn't until he had put in several years of editing other designers' work and had learned how to sketch that he developed the

courage to present his own ideas.

The sportswear he was involved with as a buyer and at John Meyer was very different from the clothes he showed at Portfolio. It consisted of tailored trousers, shirts and jackets that fit smoothly and would never be considered sloppy.

Now in his mid-thirties, he feels the world has moved on, just as his own attitudes have changed. "I hope my clothes reflect the ease of life today and the humor of it," he says. There are those who compare his exuberance with that of Kenzo, the uninhibited Japanese designer working in Paris, and who feel that in time he will be as influential.

Luis Estevez

Luis Estevez fits all the stereotypes of a fashion designer. He's dashing, good-looking, generally surrounded by glamorous people. But his head is not in the clouds and he's not disorganized as artistic temperaments tend to be. He puts together his collection as rigorously as if he were working with a computer. He is not given to violent fashion changes. He is convinced that clothes should support a woman, and he tries to build this support into all of his dresses. He thinks anything else is irresponsible.

When he started his business on Seventh Avenue in 1955, he made his big impact with the ingenuity of cut and the diversity of his necklines. He is still interested in the neckline because it gives a dress a focal point. He is aware that all women are not five feet seven inches tall and willowy. He tries to give a break to those who are shorter, plumper or have certain figure problems. "Clothes should not be far out. They should make a woman look more attractive, feel comfortable and let her personality come through," he insists.

This philosophy has given him a comfortable living in California, where he moved in the mid-1960's. For a few years he was in partnership with Eva Gabor, whose husband, Frank Jameson, introduced him to Betty Ford. Mrs. Ford is one of his prominent customers. Another is Merle Oberon, who is also one of his best friends.

Born in Cuba, he studied architecture at the University of Havana before coming to New York to do window displays for Lord & Taylor. Henry Callahan, the legendary display manager, encouraged him to design clothes. He also told him to concentrate on necklines.

Estevez recently sold the house he designed for himself in Los Angeles—between Beverly Hills and Hollywood Hills. A classic H-shaped house, it could be two thousand years old. It has tile floors, heavy wood beams and lots of mirrors. He plans to build another just like it. He enjoys building houses the way he enjoys making dresses.

Joe Famolare

Joe Famolare has always thought shoes were romantic—since he was a little boy growing up in Boston. His father was a pattern maker and designer of shoes. Joe watched him, thought what he was doing was fun and learned his trade. Later he became a shoe designer for Capezio. After that he became an executive of Marx & Newman, a large shoe company. Seven years ago he opened his own company. Since then, he has been romancing shoes.

During the energy crisis of 1973 he decided that men—and women—could move around using roller skates instead of relying on expensive gasoline. He made a line of skating shoes and tried but failed to interest people in roller-skating to school and work.

Today he advises people to get there by foot power. He devised a line of shoes with thick thermoplastic soles that he calls Get There styles. The soles aren't flat like the bottoms of most shoes. They're curved in four waves, which help dissipate the shock to the system of walking on hard pavements. In fact, they make walking a pleasure, he insists. Any-

way, he has sold three million pairs of them, which means a lot of people agree with him. Get There worked so well he designed some dressier styles with higher heels. He calls them, obviously enough, Hi There.

To romance the first group, he commissioned a song called "Get There," and includes a record of it with each pair of shoes. There's also a dance to go with it, which he hopes will become another "hustle." The idea is for stores to stage dance promotions for Get There shoes. "Every year we'll have a contest for a new song. We'll encourage all those teenage rock groups. It's dynamite," he says.

At the moment the company is shipping $100 million worth of shoes a year and it's growing. That means seventeen thousand pairs of shoes a day, made in twelve factories in Italy. The styles are shipped to a warehouse in Brattleboro, Vermont, and then sent out to three thousand stores around the country.

Joe Famolare, his wife, Sandra, and their two teenage daughters live on a farm in nearby Putney. That is, Joe lives there in between his weekly shuttle trips to his factories in Italy or his visits to customers in this country. "I'm in and out of planes all the time," he says. "It's a mad life, but I really don't mind. I was on the farm for four days at a time and I thought I'd go crazy. I like being in New York today, Italy yesterday, California tomorrow."

He has equipped his shoe designing with a philosophy. "A shoe should be more than a fashion accessory," he says. "It should be an aid to natural movement. First, it should fit and feel comfortable. Then, it should last. If it falls apart, it is no good to anyone. And third, it should be beautiful." He is sure his shoes are beautiful. "Every style we make is balanced and it makes a statement—you can't criticize our esthetics," he says confidently. "The shoe is an extension of the body. It's the one part of the costume that has to work. If it doesn't, you're in agony. Of all apparel, it's probably the hardest to make because it's three-dimensional. The rest of clothing is two-dimensional, at least until you put a body into it. You can't just cover the foot. But it doesn't cost any more to make it right. We don't have any straight lines on the inside of our shoes. Everything is curved, because that's the way the foot is shaped. And as you wear the shoe it takes on more of the shape of the foot. That's what makes it comfortable."

Besides shoes for walking and for dancing, Famolare Inc. makes sports shoes. The Boston Celtics have worn its basketball shoes, the University of Oklahoma's team its football shoes (made to function on Astroturf), and players like Clark Graebner have worn its tennis shoes. Built-in shock absorbers, self-ventilating features and angled soles make Famolare sports shoes comfortable for jogging, hiking and other activities.

Unlike most fashion, Famolare shoes have been most popular on the West Coast and are now moving East. "Possibly because people are more active in the West," Famolare speculates. They're also sold in Amsterdam, Zurich, Oslo, Copenhagen, Australia, New Zealand and Canada. And, with a beachhead recently established in Bloomingdale's, he's confident the East will fall into line.

"We're going to make it as big as Coca-Cola," he says. "We knock ourselves out for shoes. We feel the product is valid. It has good taste and some humor. We're going to go on growing. I really could stop now, but what would I do? I'm just going to go on till I drop."

The romance of shoes.

James Galanos

Small, slight and pixie-ish, James Galanos is the keeper of the couture flame in America. "I'm the last of the dinosaurs," he says wryly.

His clothes are in the grand Paris tradition. "No way to copy them," a manufacturer once observed who made his living by unauthorized "adaptations" of other people's designs. "They're much too complicated inside." Sometimes they're complicated outside too, as Galanos mixes beads and tweeds and chiffon in a pyrotechnic display for a woman who wants a suit like nobody else's. But he is best known for his almost mystical handling of chiffon in seemingly simple but superbly floating evening dresses that rival those of the acknowledged master, Alix Grès, in Paris.

People say his collections would "knock them dead in Paris," but Galanos prefers to live in California, where he has assembled a skilled work force which he refers to as "my League of Nations." It includes people from all over Europe, some from South America and a number of Japanese "who are so meticulous they can cope with anything"—even the intricacies of a standard Galanos dress.

His fanatical attention to the art of dressmaking has won him a small but devoted following of women who can afford life's luxuries. The late Rosalind Russell, one of moviedom's few achievers of best-dressed status, was a leading admirer—and a friend. But most Galanos fans lead nonprofessional lives, albeit of some elegance. "When I can't get to Paris, I find Galanos things work quite well for me," said Deeda Blair, wife of the Washington lawyer. Betsy Bloomingdale,

wife of the founder of Diners Club, and Betsy Pickering, the ex-wife of a Greek shipping magnate and a former fashion model, are typical clients. Both are tall, slender, imposing beauties who can carry off a Galanos style with élan.

"When someone says one of my styles looks like a couture dress, I feel gratified," the designer says. He is using the word "couture" in its original sense. Today, if a designer makes two collections, one casual sportswear, the other more expensive dresses, he will often refer to the higher-priced group as his couture. A store often calls its top-priced department its couture. Galanos and other purists do not use the word in this way. They mean the *haute couture* of Paris, whose work has the same relation to the usual mass-produced dress as a fine Chippendale chair does to an aluminum-and-webbing lawn chaise. An *haute couture* style can require five or six fittings and is made to order; a Galanos style is made in sizes and generally fits without any adjustment except at the hemline.

Galanos prices are comparable to those of *haute couture.* "My clothes do come in at the highest prices in this country." About the cheapest Galanos you can find at stores like Bonwit Teller costs a thousand dollars. More often women pay two thousand and three thousand for one of his dresses. "They're for women of wealth who are fussy about quality and are willing to pay for it," the designer says of his clothes. He tries to see they get taste, quality and design for their money. He designs on the model—a sketch doesn't mean too much to him. "I like to play with the fabric—the more I work with it, the more I see what it can do. The shape constantly changes and I am never satisfied—until the last day I am changing the style."

He runs his business like a one-armed paper hanger with acres of work in front of him. While Paris couturiers have armies of assistants, plus people to take care of the business end and other people to sell the clothes, Galanos supervises each facet of his collection. He does a lot of the work himself.

A notoriously retiring man, he grows eloquent when he describes his work. It is, after all, his life. To acquire the fabrics which inspire him, he travels to Europe three or four

times a year. Italy and France are his main sources. Occasionally he will have something made up specially for him, as when he ordered Tibetan prints designed by Tzaims Luksus. The fabric designer had walked over the Himalayas and spent two years in Italy. "He brought back an astonishing collection of prints," Galanos recalls. "I didn't really know what to do with them—I ordered them for their artistic value. At times I wanted to give up and just hang them on the wall. They really weren't meant for clothes. But I eventually worked it out and they proved quite successful."

After his collection is completed in Los Angeles, Galanos packs it up and takes it to New York for its presentation to the fashion world. This happens twice a year, in February for the spring-summer collection and in August for fall-winter. It is his showcase for the world. The showings are several months later than those of the designers in this country and a week or so later than the French collections. Galanos always has the last word.

After the formal presentation, which is done with no music and no commentary, the crucial phase begins: the selling. For the next two weeks he works with store buyers. Galanos is his own sales force. That's not the end of it. After the clothes get to the stores, he often arrives himself to help guide the customers to the right choice. Many rely on his judgment. Sometimes there's a formal showing in the store. He prefers to work with his clients privately, bringing along a favorite model to try on the clothes. He dislikes charity shows, where society women get involved in the modeling and the fashion presentation becomes part of an evening's festivities. "I did them early in my career," he says, "but it's a lot of extra hard work and it hardly results in much business. Buying clothes is something women take seriously and they don't want to have a lot of distractions going on."

A rather unusual fashion show was the one

presented by the Fashion Institute of Technology in the fall of 1976. It recapitulated his twenty-five years of fashion designing and it inaugurated a three months display of his clothes at the school. Earlier there had been a retrospective on the West Coast. He has become a part of fashion history.

Galanos knew he was going to be a designer since he was twelve years old. He sold sketches to Seventh Avenue manufacturers and served an apprenticeship in Paris before he opened his own house in California in 1951. Now he is the guardian of the tradition of *haute couture*. He provides the fashion world with a touchstone for the best.

Rudi Gernreich

He used psychedelic colors before the word was coined. He showed miniskirts when nobody knew how to spell the word and many people thought they were something worn by the Mouseketeers on television. He had acquired a considerable reputation in the fashion world before 1964, when the topless bathing suit made his name a household word.

Aside from Christian Dior, the name Rudi Gernreich is probably the best known outside fashion circles, and yet it's been a decade since he gave up his business and announced he would take a sabbatical for a year. He just wanted to think things through, he said at the time. Instead of just fading away, he made a public announcement because he didn't want anyone to think he had a brain tumor.

The year has stretched, and Gernreich hasn't opened a new company, but that doesn't mean he's been idle.

While he hasn't shown regular, seasonal collections on his own, he has taken part in various design projects. He's done men's clothes, quilted throws and pillows for Knoll International in the striking geometric patterns he made famous in clothes; costumes for a TV series called *Space: 1999*; clothes for the Bella Lewitzky Dance Company, a modern dance group.

Dance is his first love, and Bella Lewitzky, whose company is based in Los Angeles, credits him with far more than the costumes. She calls their association "a collaboration," and explains that she would work out the movement and he would do the "clothes that help express it." A performance of "Inscape" drew an audience of three thousand in Los Angeles and Miss Lewitzky says her collaborator was responsible for attracting a good part of it. Their newest ballet is called "Pas de Bach," and, as usual, Gernreich will use the stretch-nylon fabrics that contribute

Rudi and the dance.

to both the decor and the movement.

Ballet was the designer's first encounter with clothes. Back in the 1940's, he danced with the Lester Horton Modern Dance Troupe, where he also helped with the costumes. It was as a dancer that he developed the ideas that would please or shock the fashion world. He believes that clothes should not inhibit the body's freedom.

Looking back on the topless suit which brought him notoriety that he will probably never live down, he said, "I would do it again because I think the topless, by overstating and exaggerating a new freedom of the body, will make the moderate, right degree of freedom more acceptable." In the interest of freedom, he removed the inner structure from swimsuits as early as 1954. By the 1960's he was not only raising hemlines but constructing simple knitted tubes in psychedelic orange and red colors that served as dresses, and then adding patterned stockings to match. He banished girdles and bras to allow body freedom, and then presented the "No-bra," a simple boneless garment to provide minimal support for women who required some help.

He's applied himself to designing mater-

nity clothes, underwear and scarves, and he's back to swimsuits again, designing a collection for Berlei-Hestia, an Australian company that will market it around the world. He plans to produce the styles himself for the United States. He's doing dance clothes for Capezio and towels for kitchens and bathrooms and "tabletop stuff" for Barth & Dreyfus. He has designed furniture, but he's never found anyone to produce it because he wants it done inexpensively in plastic.

"I'm terribly anti-nostalgia," he says of his work in many design fields. "Fashion isn't just making a dress, which is a bore. It's a symbol of what people feel and think." He thinks today and tomorrow: as a designer, he tries to discern how people feel about living at the moment and in the future. He has been accused of being too Space Age–oriented.

The proof of his success is the fact that many of his ideas, denigrated at first, have passed into the fashion language. A short, compact man now in his fifties, Gernreich has always kept in touch with how young people are thinking. He lives a quiet life in the Hollywood hills and keeps his personal life private.

Gernreich's work is both sociology and art. It has a special place on the American scene.

Bill and Hazel Haire

Bill and Hazel Haire are a designing couple. They both grew up on Long Island—Bill in Forest Hills, Hazel Keleher in Jackson Heights. They met when they were in high school at life classes at the Art Students League. Both got scholarships to the Fashion Institute of Technology, and after graduation they got married.

After twenty years of marriage, they've reached the point of togetherness where one can finish the other's sentence and the other nods in approval. But until they came together at Friedricks Sport a few years ago, their careers were separate.

Hazel learned about sportswear at B.H. Wragge, an elegant sportswear house which hired her because she was a painter, and at Anne Klein, which revitalized the idea of sportswear separates. Bill worked for bridal houses and then moved into cocktail and evening clothes. For fourteen years he worked at Victoria Royal, where he designed beaded evening dresses made in Hong Kong, the last place where it was economical to produce hand-beaded numbers. "I've always hated fur coats, beaded dresses and jeweled eyeglasses," he muses today. "Fifteen thousand dresses and fourteen years later, I left."

In between jobs, Hazel retired periodically to paint. "Her feeling for color is audacious," her husband remarks. "Sometimes it knocks me out. She puts colors together no one would ever think of doing and she makes it work." Her knack for color rubs off on her clothes as well as on her canvases, height-

ening the appeal of her combinations of separates.

When she got the job designing sportswear for Henry Friedricks, a fifty-year-old coat and suit house which decided to change its design thrust, she decided to persuade her husband to quit his job making beaded dresses.

"I keep retiring—why don't you?" she told him. "Take some time off. Decide what you want to do next." Finally, she convinced him. He left the job which offered, besides security, the pleasant perks of long lunches and lots of vacation time, and stayed home. The only trouble was, after two weeks around the house he got restless. He went down to Friedricks to spend some time with his wife. Pretty soon she put him to work. In a little while they were working together officially.

"The boss was reluctant to hire him because he didn't want to be a cause for divorce—he didn't think a husband and wife could work together," Hazel says. On the contrary, the Haires recall their time together on Seventh Avenue as a "wonderful experience."

Bill quickly picked up the knack of designing sports clothes from his wife and showed a decided flair for designing coats. After a year Hazel received an offer to start her own busi-

ness and her husband carried on alone. Sportswear, it turned out, was what he wanted to do next.

"It's the only place to be if you are designing clothes today," he explains. "It's a big category that gives you the license to do almost anything. It's not limited at all. It can include coats and evening dresses and anything you want to do. In the beginning, I only knew what I learned from Hazel and she knew what she learned from Anne Klein. The systems I used were derived from hers and the styles were in the hard-edged tradition. But as I've gone along I've begun to soften the clothes. It's getting to be a blend between the dressmaking I used to do and the tailored clothes that we began with. I'm lucky, because that happens to be my natural bent and it's also what's happening in clothes. It's still considered sportswear, but when you take out the linings and the stiff construction, it turns into something else."

When Hazel's business venture foundered, she didn't panic. She went back to her oils and canvas happily enough and devoted herself to furnishing the Haires' new Park Avenue apartment. She has the luxury of being able to approach any new fashion venture "very carefully." Her husband's career is flourishing.

Halston

Near the top—perhaps at the very pinnacle—of the fashion world stands a tall, classically good-looking man in a black turtleneck sweater, exuding charm and good will. Roy Halston Frowick he is, better known as simply Halston, born a Midwesterner but at ease anywhere.

A nod from Halston, and a fashion is flashed around the world. Not that he's ever dictatorial about it. It just happens that his name carries authority. Let him revive the twin sweater set in cashmere, tying the cardigan around the neck like a scarf, and myriad fashionable women adopt the look. More recently there was the strapless dress and the slightly askew or asymmetric V neckline. Both traveled as far as Paris, let alone all over the United States.

Halston operates from two power bases. One is his boutique and custom salon on Madison Avenue and 68th Street—he refers to it as his "uptown" site—and the other is on Seventh Avenue, in the heart of the garment district. There he makes the clothes that are sold in stores throughout the country. "Uptown" is where he fits the prestigious women who can afford made-to-order clothes.

There are a host of other Halston products, some thirty in all, including perfume, make-up, towels, sheets, relatively inexpensive shirts and skirts, raincoats and furs.

"The designing isn't difficult—you get an idea like the asymmetric neckline and you adapt it to all the different things—but the meetings are so time-consuming," he says. Indeed, he makes it sound easy. Part of his charm is the effortless way he goes about his life.

He was the first in his family to have anything to do with fashion.

His father did construction work for military camps, and during World War II he went to school "all over the Midwest—Missouri, Indiana, the Ozarks—ending up in Evansville, Indiana." After attending the Art Institute of Chicago, he opened a millinery shop there. "Fran Allison, who was part of the Kukla, Fran and Ollie show on television, came in the first week to buy some hats, a Chicago fashion editor did a full-page story on me, and I was an immediate success," he recalls. He had met Lilly Daché in Chicago, and when he came to New York she gave him a job. Marilyn Monroe and Jacqueline

Halston and friends (clockwise from upper left): posing with Andy Warhol; welcoming Apollonia Van Ravenstein and Michael Bennett; making an entrance with Princess Diane de Beauvau; kissing Martha Graham; escorting Bianca Jagger; chatting with Andy, Diana Vreeland, and Victor Hugo; mugging with Margaux Hemingway; receiving an award from Abe Beame; smooching with Barbara Allen; hamming with Pat Ast.

Kennedy, then the young senator's wife, came in for hats and veils.

He was doing the headdresses for a Du Pont wedding party and was asked to fit them at Bergdorf Goodman, where the dresses for the bride and her attendants were being made. "Bergdorf was maybe the most snobbish place to shop and they couldn't get over the fact that I was asked to do the veils, not them, so they asked me to work for them," is the way he tells it.

Thus began his career in earnest. Not only did he get to meet and work with "the most incredible clientele," but he traveled to Europe with the store's top buyers. He met all the couturiers (the store was one of the biggest buyers of couture clothes), including Balenciaga, his idol.

By the end of the 1960's not only were hats waning, but they were practically obsolete. He tried a clothes collection at Bergdorf. He wanted to bridge the gap between couture clothes and ready-to-wear. The styles had "a

little better workmanship than ready-to-wear, a little younger look than couture clothes." He left Bergdorf's soon after this experiment.

In a new shop on 68th Street he showed a collection on his own that was supposed to be a boutique collection. "My first client was Babe Paley [Mrs. William Paley, wife of the broadcasting chief and one of the country's best-dressed women]. She had been my client at Bergdorf and she wanted to give me a good send-off. My second client was Jane Engelhard [Mrs. Charles Engelhard, wife of the precious-metals tycoon], who also wanted to give me a break. They both came

the morning after my first show and I knew I was in business." See how easy it was?

Once established on his own, Halston proceeded to make his big contribution to fashion: he cleaned it up. The 1960's had ended in a whirl of fringe, scarves, leathers, patchwork and other eccentricities. Halston brought back a pure simplicity. First came his cashmere sweaters. Then the shirtwaist dress in Ultrasuede. He explains it this way: "For many years, before the 1960's, the fashionable woman showed her riches on her body. Her carefully tailored suit was set off by a beautiful pin. Her jewelry was lavish. So were her accessories. Then the pendulum

swung. During the day, at least, the society woman didn't want to stand out. She wanted to blend in with everybody else. High style was finished for day. The mood of fashion was more relaxed, as women didn't want to draw attention to themselves. At night, of course, it is different. In private homes, yachts or resorts, people still want to dress up. In a way, it is an underground society, because you don't see it so much in public."

The theory doesn't apply to social women only. Halston's clients include rock stars, actresses and executives like Katharine Graham, the publisher of the Washington *Post.* Another of his fans is Martha Graham: "She came to me when she was receiving some award and didn't have anything to wear. I fell in love with her immediately, and I've done things for her performers as well as for her private life." Liz Taylor wanted him to do the dress she would wear to the Academy Awards ceremony. "She called and said, 'Is this really Halston?' I said, 'Is this really Elizabeth Taylor?' We both laughed and we've been friends ever since. She asked me to come to Hollywood for the Academy Awards. I'd always wanted to go and I thought, What better way than with Liz Taylor?"

Underneath the charm and gallantry is a very clear thinker. Halston worries about female figures as well as about the introduction of new styles: "You have to have something for the woman who is overweight—a loose tunic and pants is good because it elongates the body. You have to have something for the woman with hips—the princess line works for her. Caftans are fine for the woman whose figure isn't perfect. You have to have dresses for all kinds of people—short ones and tall ones. You have to consider bodies before you get into innovations. I do story boards, like they do in the theater, before I even begin a collection.

"For most women, the one-piece dress is more orderly, easier to handle than separates. Most women don't want to muss their hair—a back zipper is good for them.

"There are many different clients—one needs pretty, ladylike clothes, another likes the extremes because she wants to be noticed. The third is the one with discerning taste, her own style—she ultimately makes fashion."

95

Cathy Hardwick

Cathy Hardwick is Korean, which was crucial to her becoming a fashion designer. When she came to California to live and, eventually, marry, she had trouble finding clothes that fit her. Like many Oriental women, she couldn't fit into Western sizes. She remembers: "In a regular size ten, the waistline would be down to my hips. In the junior sections of stores, the waist would be under my bust. Nothing seemed to fit me ever, so I started making clothes for myself. Then I started making them for my friends.

"I thought it would be nice to sell them to a store, and I asked a friend how one did this. She told me to see the buyer. The first buyer I went to, at Joseph Magnin, looked at the things I brought her and ordered them. That's the way everything has happened to me—very unplanned."

Her next step was opening a small boutique of her own in San Francisco. She found a couple of girls who could sew and went into business. After about a year, a man named Alvin Duskin came in and asked her to work for him. He was a manufacturer in San Francisco who was fascinated by New York, where he felt everything in fashion began. He asked her to open a design studio for him in New York and so she moved East.

"Soon I got the biggest kick out of seeing girls in New York wearing my dresses. They were teeny little mini dresses, all in dusty pastel colors. I got sick of them after a while."

She was designing sample collections for other manufacturers when a buyer for Bloomingdale's came by and asked her to make some dresses for the store. They sold well and Cathy Hardwick found herself in the manufacturing business. "It wasn't planned," she repeats. "It was accidental."

The business flourished and in 1975 she bought a brownstone on the East Side where she lives with her youngest child, Anthony, who is twelve years old. She has two daughters in California, one in Paris, and has long been separated from her husband.

"Women should dress to be happy, to be comfortable," she says. "If you feel self-conscious when you go out, you are probably wearing something wrong. Whether you are dressing for the supermarket or for a big party, if you feel awkward, you are not dressed properly. There are no other rules any more."

Taste and style have nothing to do with price, she believes. It is quite possible to pick up bits and pieces in Army surplus stores and end up looking fabulous. Sometimes a tiny person like herself can look marvelous in a big dress that in the abstract sounds wrong for her. "If you feel right, you are right," she tells people, adding, "It's better to underdress than overdress."

Her clothes are diverse, but they are mainly planned for women who go to work. Business clothes, she calls them, "because I hardly know anyone who stays home."

She is not averse to praising other designers: her favorites include Chanel, Sonia Rykiel, whom she calls "today's version of Chanel," Zandra Rhodes and Jean Muir.

"It sounds as if I just admire women designers, but that's not true," she says. "I like Geoffrey Beene and some of the things Halston does and Missoni and Calvin Klein, and I have a great Ralph Lauren trench coat that I will probably wear for the rest of my life."

She obviously is in love with fashion, but not too serious about clothes. "What I aim at is to inject a small touch of humor," she says. She thinks her clothes are young, but not adolescent-looking. "Young clothes don't have to be in bad fabrics and they don't have to be badly made," she says. "They don't have to be only for women in their twenties either." In fact, she likes to think of her things as being for women in their thirties. But a lot of teenagers wear them too. It is a question of spirit and attitude—her own as well as the wearer's.

Like other fashion designers, she's branching into other fields. Her first dinnerware designs for Mikasa have just been completed.

Holly Harp

When Holly Harp was designing a recent collection, she spotted a red chiffon scrap of fabric on the floor and pinned it to the sleeve of a dress she was making. Because it trailed off like a flame, she found a blowtorch and burned the hemline to heighten the effect. She liked the contrast of the charred edges with the red chiffon, so she burned the hems of a number of other styles as well.

For the same collection, she found a box of old French lace collars and designed a group of soft, cuddly wool dresses to go with them. The dresses ended up with an angelic look, which pleased her exceedingly.

"That's what my clothes are all about," she explained. "They're a release, entertainment. When you put on the lace-collar dress, you're an angel. When you wear the burned one, you're a siren. You're just having a moment of fun, and nobody's the worse for it."

She doesn't think much when designing. For her, it is almost a visceral process.

"My clothes have to do with the joy of being a female: to be pretty, desirable, decorative—all the things we are trying to get away from with women's liberation. I deal in nostalgia. I'm a romantic and my things are reactionary. They have nothing to do with modern life.

"Fifty years from now they will have vanished, like the hoop skirt and high heels. Meanwhile, they are beautiful. At the end of the day, when you get out of your work clothes, you put them on and you escape for a second or two. People still want to be pretty, and I see no harm in it."

Holly Harp does her designing in Hollywood, where she opened a shop ten years ago that attracted women who remembered the glory days of the silver screen. With chiffon and satin she made dresses that recreated the glamour era for such women as Tony Curtis's wife, Leslie, and Harry Belafonte's wife, Julia. The shop became a magnet for women seeking offbeat clothes,

Holly and her son, Tommy.

among them Diahann Carroll ("She's flaw-less"), Joanne Woodward ("Extraordinary"), Ali MacGraw ("Boy, she has taste"), Jane Fonda, Barbra Streisand and Liza Minnelli. Faye Dunaway came in and bought a dress one morning and was married in it at City Hall that afternoon.

Naturally, word got around outside the Hollywood community. Today she runs a large factory which produces and ships her clothes to ninety stores around the country.

It's a heady life for the girl from Buffalo, New York, who dropped out of Radcliffe after one year and went to Acapulco to make san-dals. "I earned a hundred dollars a month, which was all I needed to live—I got taken to dinner a lot."

People kept stopping her and asking about the clothes she wore, and she found she was getting a kick out of it. She decided to become a designer and went back to school. She got a degree in art from North Texas State Univer-sity, where she minored in costume design. She also met her husband, Jim, there. After graduation, they headed for California.

It was the era of boutiques, so with $10,000 borrowed from her father in Buffalo the two set up shop. Within two months she got preg-

nant. "In the beginning it wasn't too much fun. Every morning I would take my baby to the nurse so I could work in the shop, but everything survived—except the marriage," she recalls. Jim Harp is still her business partner, taking care of sales, but the couple separated two years ago.

Today she's far more successful than she ever thought she'd be, but her schedule is grueling. When she's working on a collection, she wakes up as early as 4:30 a.m. ("I can only sleep four or five hours"), goes swimming in her pool ("I try to wait until the sun comes up") and sits down at her dining room table from six to seven-thirty to take up the day's business. She breakfasts with her son, Tommy, then sets off for her factory. Her model comes in at 10 a.m. and she fits clothes on her. She tries to remember to call the grocery before noon "because they won't deliver after that."

Her days have their highs. "When I make something that looks gorgeous, I get all excited. If it looks wretched, well, you just have to write it off."

She considers herself lucky. "I consider myself an artist. I'm more concerned with aesthetics than commerce. And I have the privilege of expressing myself all the time. It's a wonderful way to go through life."

Edith Head

"I've dressed the great beauties of the world," said the brisk little woman behind the big dark-rimmed sunglasses that have become her signature. Dressed in a simple no-nonsense suit, she ticked off some of their names: Clara Bow, Mae West, Joan Crawford, Dorothy Lamour ("I did the first sarong for her—I copied it from a native's style"), Jean Harlow, Barbara Stanwyck, Faye Dunaway ("If she hadn't been an actress, she could have been a designer"), Grace Kelly ("An extraordinary woman—if I had to name a favorite, it would have to be her"), Marilyn Monroe, Carole Lombard, Elizabeth Taylor ("Possibly the most beautiful human being who ever lived and the most fun to be with—did you know she was an extraordinary cook?").

The speaker pauses for breath. The list is endless. Edith Head recalls the women of glamour with a schoolteacher's precision. Indeed, she was a schoolteacher for several years before she entered Hollywood's glamorous kingdom as a sketch artist. She started with Paramount, where she worked with Travis Banton, the favorite designer of Marlene Dietrich and Carole Lombard.

"The star was a star in those days," she said. "She wore real fur, real jewels. If we made a beaded dress for Carole, it would be hand-beaded—we had rooms of women who would be working on it. It wouldn't occur to me then to worry about what anything cost. We made beautiful clothes. We had women stand in line to see what Joan Crawford was wearing."

Initially she didn't design for the stars. Her first design was a costume for an elephant in a Cecil B. De Mille film. What does an elephant wear? A blanket of flowers, "But you have to be careful—elephants eat certain flowers." After the elephant came Westerns, where she did mostly men's clothes and characters such as grandmothers "and the rest of the people in the background—the big designers didn't want to bother about them."

Her first major picture was *She Done Him Wrong,* with Mae West and Cary Grant. "I got it because Banton was in Paris looking at the collections and buying fabrics. It was Cary's first picture. Mae said, 'I like that tall, handsome one—let's get him,' and they did. I dressed them both." After that came almost a thousand pictures—"Nine hundred eighty-seven and a half," she says in her precise manner, explaining, "One wasn't finished."

"My job was to change people into something they weren't—it was a cross between camouflage and magic. We asked the public to look at the same star over and over and pretend she was a different person. In *Rear Window* Grace Kelly was a fashion editor and had to look chic. In *Country Girl* she was a dowdy housewife with no taste. In *High Society* she had to look expensive. The same body, but three different characters. With hair, make-up and costume changes, we helped persuade the public that she was these different people."

Along the way, she learned what colors, fabrics and patterns can do to the human body. She learned how to make anyone look ten years younger, ten pounds thinner. Some of her basic tenets:

Wear darker colors in the danger area. ("The danger area is fat, since you can't be too thin.")

Never wear shiny fabrics or bold patterns in areas where you are large.

Heavy people should never fit their clothes too tightly. "Never put tight pants over a big bottom."

Few women can look at themselves in a mirror and be honest about what they see, she has found. It is difficult to dissociate one's body from one's face. Her suggestion: Put a paper bag over your head with two holes cut out for the eyes so you can see. Then look at yourself in a mirror. You may decide you shouldn't put a belt with a heavy buckle over a thick middle. Or you may see that the length you are wearing is an awkward one.

following page, Edith and the dress she designed for Elizabeth Taylor in A Place in the Sun.

"There was a time when women knew these things automatically because being well dressed was part of being a woman. Today anything goes," she says. "Fashion negates the rules."

The golden age of the movies is over too. Films today focus on disasters or action. The big stars are men. Edith Head has gone on to other things too. She designs uniforms for Pan American Airlines and the women in the Coast Guard. For Vogue Patterns she does clothes women can sew themselves.

She lives in a rambling ranch house in Cold Water Canyon, five minutes from Beverly Hills, with her husband, Wiard Ihnen, an architect, and doesn't mourn the vanished world of glamour. But she's had a pin made of miniatures of the eight Oscar statues she's won, starting with *The Heiress* in 1949 and ending with *The Sting* in 1973. That shows she's been part of it.

109

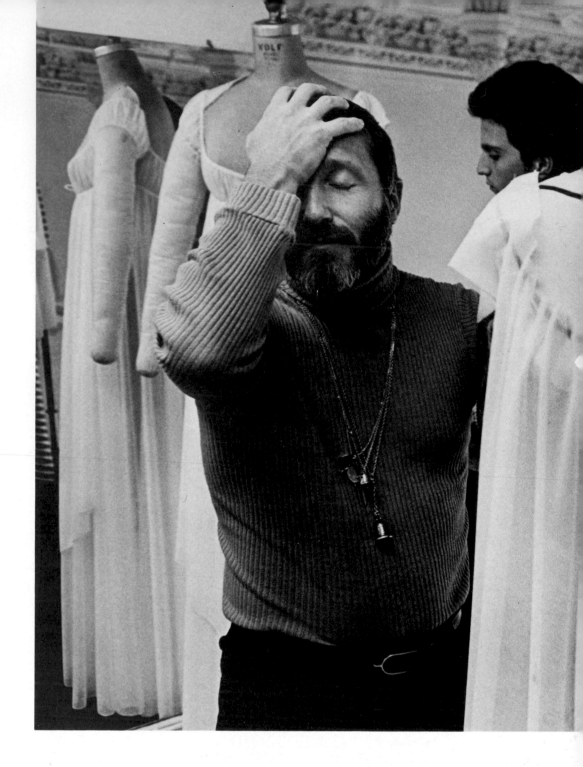

Stan
Herman

Seventh Avenue is but a short block away from Broadway, and Stan Herman has worked them both. As a singer, he faked the voices of Andy Williams, Elvis Presley and others on pirated records; he appeared in *La Plume de Ma Tante* on Broadway. He wanted to be an opera singer.

His first jobs as a designer—they often overlapped his stints as a singer—were disastrous. Sometimes the firm went out of business. Sometimes he was fired. But in 1960 he hit his stride. He went to work for Mr. Mort (the company was later taken over by Russ Togs, a giant apparel manufacturer, where it served as the prestige fashion flagship).

He was caught up in the exuberance of the 1960's. He became a celebrity. His tent dresses were in the vanguard of fashion. His sexy wrap dress was a precursor of Diane Von Furstenberg's. When pants began to move into the mainstream, he showed his models wearing dresses over pants and that became the fashion-of-the-moment. Then the

bubble burst. The 1960's were over.

The 1970's began with the introduction of the midi, the long skirt that followed the mini, and many women turned their backs on fashion, even the inexpensive variety. Mr. Mort went out of business.

Stan Herman was forced to find another approach. Instead of designing clothes for one firm, he opened a design studio. He would do anything—it was impossible to know where his name would appear next. As a free lance, he designed loungewear, which he had begun to do when he was at Mr. Mort. He made a dress line for Bendel's Studio. He did a collection of fake fur coats and jackets—

and presented it at the Central Park Zoo. The singer may have retired, but the showman was still there.

And then he discovered a new field, career apparel. These are the clothes that people wear at work—often undistinguished, often years behind the current fashion. He's worked for banks, airlines and McDonald's, concerning himself with the décor as well as the uniforms.

Sometimes he feels a twinge that he is not in the middle of the garment industry, "in the hot center of things." Life off Seventh Avenue has its compensations, but it's not the same as being a star.

113

Carol Horn

The mop of curls that swirl around Carol Horn's head is not an attempt to suggest the Afro or some other trendy hairdo. It happens to be the way her hair grows naturally, and after years of trying to tame the curls or make them lie flat, she decided to live with them. When some strands of gray began to turn up, she left them alone too. It suits her, and it doesn't interfere for a minute with her free, gamine air.

For a long time, Carol Horn was identified as the keeper of the ethnic look in fashion, retaining as she did some of the exuberance of the gypsy and peasant clothes that were a signature of the 1960's. She imported crinkly cotton fabrics from India which she used in loose, smocklike blouses. Her skirts wrapped and tied. She mixed up prints and developed patchwork effects in sweaters. Nothing looked as if it was planned to go together.

But today Carol Horn's gone beyond ethnic. "I really don't know what it means any more," she says. "What counts now is clothes." What she is most interested in about clothes is their versatility. She likes things that can feel comfortable during the day or at night. She likes dresses that change their shape by the way they are tied around the body. She likes parts that can be piled one on

115

top of each other to fit the temperature or the mood.

Most of all, she feels that clothes should express the personality of the woman wearing them. She wants women to feel free to experiment with colors and shapes they've never tried before—it's part of the liberation movement. Actually, she didn't always feel this way. She used to believe that a woman's role was to get married and wear fine clothes. She married when she was quite young. When the marriage broke up she looked for a way to support herself. She wasn't really prepared for anything, but she had studied art at Boston University and at Columbia. She landed a job as the only girl on the display staff at Macy's and, through contacts she made there, began to design clothes in the late 1960's.

Her philosophy began to evolve. "The breaking down of the status thing in clothes is great," she said in 1971. "People no longer have to dress the way their neighbors dress to feel secure. They don't have to build their egos by owning oodles of clothes." The following year she said, "I used to have to wear something different every day; now I find a few comfortable things and I stay with them." She was developing confidence. A few years later, now in her own company called Carol

right page, Carol and Giorgio Sant' Angelo at a Washington party.

Horn's Habitat, she was saying things like, "Women have the freedom to do anything they want," and "If someone takes clothes too seriously, it just means they spend a lot of money."

Not that she puts clothes down. They can be liberating, a means of expression, she believes. "Sometimes I see a girl of fifteen who understands this, sometimes it's a women of fifty. If I have a mission, it's to encourage women to cultivate their own style and taste. I try to make it easier by providing the materials, but it's up to the woman to make dressing herself an adventure."

As she designs her clothes, or as she presents them to store buyers, she tries them on, she moves in them. This is one of the advantages of being a woman designer. "You have to get into the things to know what works and what doesn't," she explains.

She lives, not too far from her office, in a studio filled with mementos of her travels—statues, wall hangings, ivory tables—and myriad plants. "It's a potpourri," she says. "It's very comfortable." Her collections, too, are assemblages of miscellaneous styles. They provide many options from which a woman can select the ones that pertain to her.

Charles James

Charles James is one of fashion's living legends. In the days when couture, or made-to-order, clothes dominated the fashion world, he dressed the fabled women whose names turned up repeatedly in the world's society columns and magazines. Elizabeth de Cuevas, Millicent Rogers, Doris Duke, Austine Hearst, Mrs. Harrison Williams and Gertrude Lawrence were among his clients (patrons would be a better word—buying a dress from him was like commissioning a painting). Sometimes they waited for months for the dress to be completed. "I spent my life making fashion an art form," he says.

But almost from the beginning he had a dual vision. He saw the couture salon as a design laboratory, where fashion would be created for women with the taste for originality and the money to support the artist who would give it to them. At the same time, he envisioned adaptation of couture techniques to factory production. He was probably the first couture designer to mass-produce inexpensive copies of his own work. In 1929 he sold hats to Best & Co., a New York department store. In the same year he invented a spiral dress with no side or back seams. Five years later he put a zipper in it and sold it for $10 at wholesale to the same store.

The designer cherishes such accolades as this, from Pavel Tchelitchew, in 1958: "I am convinced that if there is one genius in high fashion in our period, it is you, with your Pythagorean 'attitude' translated into the volume of sleeves and the width of skirts."

He makes lists of clients he would have liked to dress (Gertrude Stein, Greta Garbo, David Bowie, Mick Jagger), and he revives such styles as the ribbon cape he made in 1936 or the tucked-front dress in 1939. (A copy of the latter that he found in a thrift shop was much more complicated and less graceful then the original.)

"I'm the only American who challenged Paris," he says. "I sold originals at the same prices as Schiaparelli and Vionnet. I could set up a couture salon in Paris, but what would I do there? Jean Cocteau, everybody I know, is dead."

Charles James had couture salons in London in the late 1920's and in Paris in the 1930's. In the 1940's he set up the custom department at Elizabeth Arden, and in the 1950's he did wholesale collections on Seventh Avenue for Samuel Winston and William Popper. He designed baby clothes and maternity clothes and made dresses for Korvettes. He worked briefly with Halston in the 1960's. Somenow the wholesale ventures never turned out right. He couldn't adapt himself to Seventh Avenue methods and he was unable to hold his own on Seventh Avenue. He was called a genius—and a wild man.

There were plenty of honors. His clothes found their way into museums, justifying his contention that fashion was art. He has lectured at schools and has always attracted disciples. Like a sculptor, he thinks of fashion in the round. His clothes have their own shape; they do not depend on the shape of the person wearing them. He has made grand ball gowns and simple dresses, like the spiral one. A white satin eiderdown-padded jacket he made in 1938 is a precursor of today's popular ski jacket. He understands the subtlety of seaming: waistlines come up higher in front and dip in the back to create a more graceful line.

There was a retrospective showing of his work at the Electric Circus, the New York discotheque, in 1969, when he was sixty-three years old. Since then he has lived in three cluttered rooms in the Hotel Chelsea, sorting his mementos, passing on his work methods to students.

From his voluminous files he pulls out a letter from James Galanos: "You have always been in my eyes a Fashion God—a simple James creation is worth the whole output of a Seventh Avenue year's work." His eyes glow as he scans the paper. He transcends the shabby surroundings. He has had a vision of fashion as a high art and some people have acknowledged it. What does it matter that he has not achieved any monetary success, or that his name is not a household word? He will preserve what he can. The future will understand.

Mr. John

Two aging men sit in the chandeliered living room of the *haute bourgeoise* apartment house on Central Park West, where the elevators are still manned and visitors are announced. Gazing across the park over the petunias blooming in the window boxes, the short, chunky man who calls himself Mr. John announces, "There were mansions there on Fifth Avenue, not the condominiums you see now, and I made up my mind when I was little boy I'd get into all of them, through the front door."

Memories and fantasies intermingle in the room and knock against each other as the raucous squawks of five parrots interrupt the momentary silence.

"That one's Josephine," Mr. John observes.

"She was Napoleon for five years until she laid an egg on Peter's bed." Peter Brandon, né Matthias Peter Brandon Ammann, and business partner of Mr. John, grimaces.

"Peter's the bird person—they bite the hell out of me." says Mr. John. "I like dogs."

More screams from Josephine, né Napoleon.

The mansions across the park stimulate the flow of nostalgia. "I had a mother who was a milliner, Madame Laurel she was called. I was born in Europe. My mother was German, my father was Italian. His name was Juan Pico. That's my name too, but they changed it to John when we came here and I went to school in New Rochelle."

Juan is Italian?

Mr. John shrugs. He goes back to the mansions. "I wanted to have my own house, so I borrowed five hundred dollars from my sister. I needed five hundred dollars more, so

I walked into the Chase National Bank and told the manager I wanted to borrow money. He said he couldn't lend it to me—I was too young, and making hats wasn't a masculine occupation. But he'd send his wife to me. If she liked my hats, she would have five hundred dollars with her to give me. That was Mr. Rockefeller.''

Which Mr. Rockefeller?

"It wasn't Winthrop. Or Nelson. Peter, which Rockefeller was it?''

"I'll look it up.''

"Mary Pickford—she was one of my first customers. Peter and I spent many days at Pickfair. We were lucky. We had the chance to see the inner workings of Hollywood in the great days. Kitty Miller, Bobo Rockefeller, Marlene Dietrich—they were all my friends.

"Mother told me I should get paid for taking the trimming off, instead of for putting it on. Writers came along and they called me an eccentric. They said I was a mad hatter. That isn't true. I always loved classic styles. I was conservative, though I had a theatrical flair.

"Noël Coward said you had to have a focus in your shows. So we dressed up this actress in a black hat and a veil and a rented sable coat. We called her Madame Alvarez and said she was a rich woman from Spain. Soon everybody was talking about her. But she was invented.''

The names float around the room. Judy Garland. Vivien Leigh. Garbo. Christian Dior.

"We opened a special salon in California to take care of the movie trade. I did eight hundred films—*Shanghai Express, Painted Veil, Gone With the Wind.* California was the sexy part of the business, New York was quieter, the society women were conservative.''

"John's interested in making clothes that sell for about a hundred and twenty-five. You have to do that to survive,'' interjects Brandon.

John doesn't seem terribly interested. He changes the subject. "If it's pure and well done, it has no age,'' he says. "A woman should be able to go into her closet and pick out anything that suits her from the last thirty-five years. I'm with it. I want to do something new and fabulous. I also paint. I paint on sculpted linen. I'm rather pleased with how it's going.''

The silence is punctuated by the squawks of the birds. Old milliners live in the same world as old movie stars.

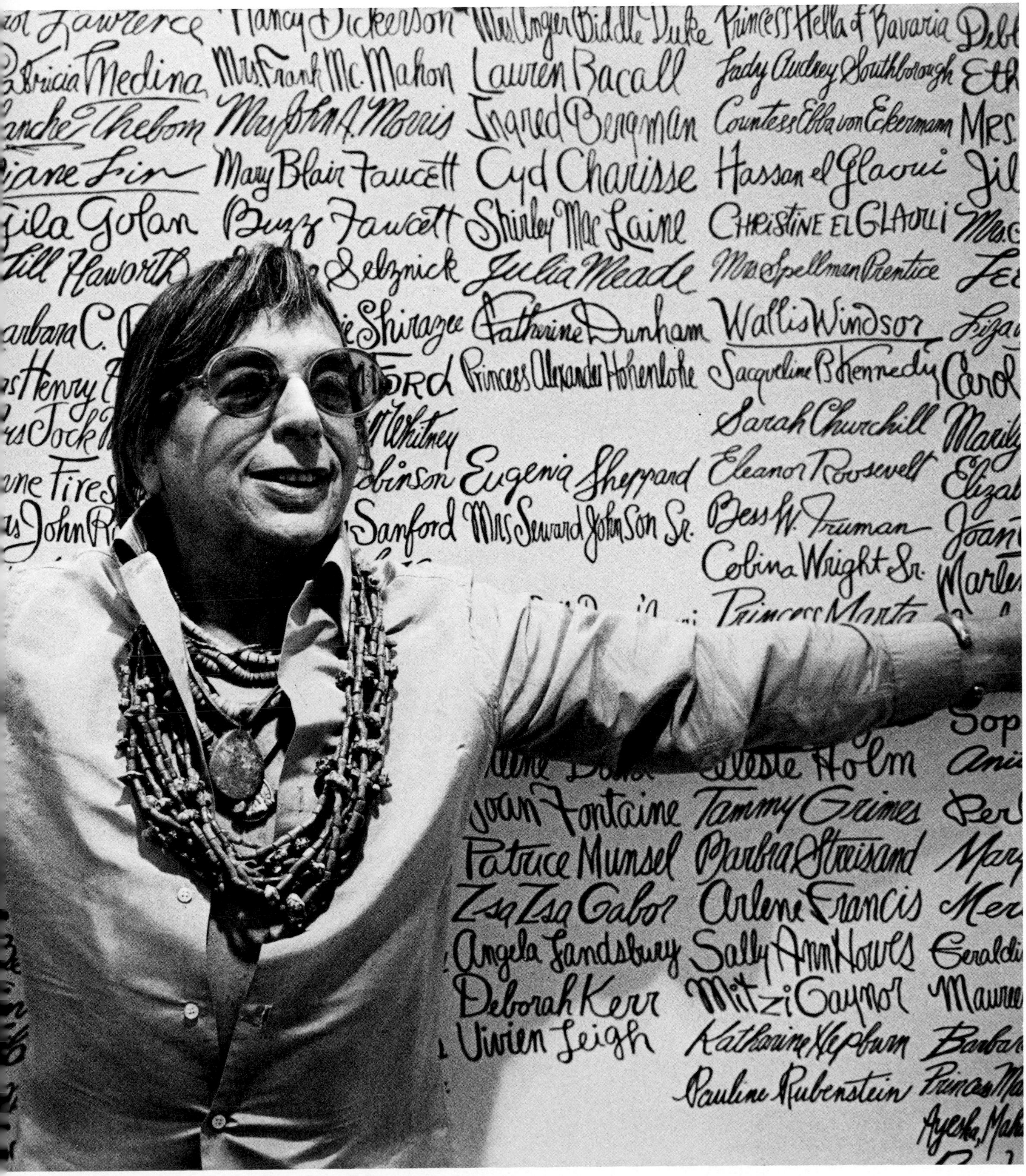

Nancy Dickerson
Mrs. Angier Biddle Duke
Princess Hella of Bavaria
Mrs. Frank McMahon
Lauren Bacall
Lady Audrey Southborough
Mrs. John A. Morris
Ingrid Bergman
Countess Ebba von Eckermann
Mary Blair Fawcett
Cyd Charisse
Hassan el Glaoui
Buzz Fawcett
Shirley MacLaine
Christine el Glaoui
Julia Meade
Mrs. Spellman Prentice
Katherine Dunham
Wallis Windsor
Princess Alexander Hohenlohe
Jacqueline B. Kennedy
Sarah Churchill
Eugenia Sheppard
Eleanor Roosevelt
Mrs. Seward Johnson Sr.
Bess W. Truman
Cobina Wright Sr.
Joan Fontaine
Tammy Grimes
Patrice Munsel
Barbra Streisand
Zsa Zsa Gabor
Arlene Francis
Angela Landsbury
Sally Ann Howes
Deborah Kerr
Mitzi Gaynor
Vivien Leigh
Katharine Hepburn
Pauline Rubenstein

Betsey Johnson

She emerged in the swinging sixties to break down the barriers that made clothes stiff and unrelenting. She captured the spirit of the flower children, of the do-your-own-thing generation. She was a youthquake unto herself.

Things slowed down in the 1970's for Betsey Johnson—as the times changed, tailored clothes replaced madness and the young people grew outwardly sedate.

Now she's revving up again. She lives in a vast loft in a commercial area of New York, midway between Wall Street and the garment center. Her work area is separated by screens from her living space, which includes a kitchen on a platform and, in a corner, a tub surrounded by red curtains. Favorite photos and mementos are taped in red to her refrigerator. There's a parrot in a cage, surrounded by a lot of trees in pots, in what she calls her "tropical corner."

The only separate room in the loft is occupied by Lulu, her two-year-old daughter, for whom she designs mini versions of her grown-up styles.

The clothes she's making are in the same spirit of the things she made in the 1960's. "They have a sense of humor, I hope," she said. "That's what separates them from other similar things. There's some attention to detail, maybe in stitching in a different-color thread, or in the print I use. Most of all, they have to fit snugly—my work is all in the cut. If they are too big, it's all over and I know the horrors of things being too small."

Her clothes are really an amalgam of T-shirt and peasant dresses. It's the tops that must fit snugly—the bottoms can flounce all over the place. Betsey Johnson has always had an eye for peasant styles. She also likes mad, billowing odd-shaped pants.

But the most unusual feature of her clothes

Max Blag, Betsey and Lulu picnic on the roof.

is their price. "This stuff at high prices would be wrong," she observed. "The clothes must be affordable. They're always special clothes and, in that sense, timeless, but I don't see them as being expensive."

What she considers affordable is a knit top for $10, a dress for $28 to $35—nothing higher than $40. Kids' clothes should be less—T-shirts should sell for $4 to $6. To accomplish this, she is having them made in Hong Kong and using Taiwan for some crocheted things and for handwork. Her associate is Michael Milea, with whom she has collaborated before and who has close ties in the Far Eastern market.

Betsey Johnson was born in Wethersfield, Connecticut, and grew up interested in both dancing and art. She ran a dance school when she was in high school and bought the lamé and sequin fabrics the mothers would sew into costumes their children would wear at recitals. She went to Pratt Institute for a year, then to Syracuse University and, in 1964, won a guest editorship at *Mademoiselle* magazine.

"We all went to London that year. It was swinging London, with the mods and the rockers. We felt like Cinderellas. The world

128

was opening up to us.''

She worked as an illustrator for about a year, made clothes for the editors of the magazine, and wasn't really thinking about becoming a designer when she was offered a job at Paraphernalia, which tried to capture the frenetic feeling and the excitement of the 1960's.

"Brigitte Bardot was my idea of an interesting woman and Rudi Gernreich was the only designer I had respect for—he knew what he was doing,'' she recalls.

She was married for a few years to John Cale, a rock musician who was a member of the Velvet Underground. Their divorce was amicable and they're still good friends. When she was thirty-three, she yearned to have a child, but she and Lulu's father separated four months after Lulu was born. "He was a sculptor and we never got married. I went through living alone for about a year and being completely responsible for Lulu. Of course, there was a loneliness period, but after I was happy and peaceful about myself, I met Maxwell. He's a writer and very supportive of my work. He's not competitive. I realize I need my own space, my separateness, and he needs his. We don't plan to marry."

Betsey Johnson is in control of her life and her work. "I feel I've undergone a rebirth,'' she said, "I'm doing what I want to do."

Bill Kaiserman

The name first appeared in hats—men's hats—about ten years ago. Then it turned up in leather and suede safari jackets, shorts and trousers—still for men. Soon there were cashmere sweaters and silk shirts. And finally the safari jacket grew into a whole new category of clothes for men—the leisure suit. It catapulted Bill Kaiserman into the top rank of men's fashion designers in the early 1970's and was as widely copied as Yves Saint Laurent's peasant styles were to be later in the decade. For many men all over the country the leisure suit became a way of life. It bridged the gap between formal business attire and casual sports clothes and it caught on so quickly it became a cliché.

The name on the label of all his clothes is "Rafael," chosen because it had a classy sound to Mr. Kaiserman, who thought it would look better in print than his own. Soon after the success of the leisure suit, he used the same label for women's clothes. He started with tailored styles, because tailoring was what he knew best, but soon moved on to softer things.

"You can be much freer in designing for women," he says. "With men's clothes, you start with something imaginative, and then you have to cut it back so it won't seem 'too much.' The end result is something fairly classic. With women's clothes there are fewer restrictions. You can start from any base. The clothes can go towards the body or away from the body. I'm still learning how to use that freedom. With men, there are just a few shapes that are acceptable; there is less room for fantasy. You have to be realistic."

A man, he believes, looks best when his clothes are not too well put together. A woman looks best when "you can see the shape of her body." Male or female, his typ-

ical customer is probably in the thirty- to forty-five-year-old bracket, in fairly good shape, with a youthful outlook. "They want to look young without dressing like a kid," he says.

His customers not only are aware of quality but can afford to pay for it. Typically, a Rafael suit for men sells for around $300, a woman's style a trifle less at $275. They're found at places like Bonwit Teller, I. Magnin and Neiman-Marcus. Sales volume of his women's clothes is rapidly approaching that of the longer-established men's styles, and together they provide Bill Kaiserman and his wife, Milly, with an enviable life style. They live in

a house on Beekman Place which they rent but hope to buy. They travel to Europe, where the clothes are produced every other month, and they have just ordered a 60-foot ocean-going boat in which they hope to cruise around the Mediterranean, the Caribbean or Canada as the spirit moves them.

Milly was an actress who appeared as the body-paint girl in the television show *Laugh In,* and was a dancer with Carol Burnett. She was working in a clothing store in Beverly Hills between acting jobs when Bill Kaiserman came in to sell his men's sportswear styles. He took her to lunch and flew back to Los Angeles six or seven weekends in a row to see her. Six years ago they were married.

"I enjoy where I am in life," she says. "I feel I'm a part of Bill's business. I tell him what I like and what I don't like. I'm happy being a homemaker." She mixes a potion for her husband each morning containing lecithin, bran, wheat germ, brewer's yeast, skimmed milk and banana, which fills him up so he doesn't feel like eating anything until 4 p.m. The Kaisermans consider themselves health freaks. "I spend an hour every day exercising," he says. "I love to lift weights—I'll get an idea for a dress while I'm doing it. If I can't be the biggest women's designer, I will certainly be the strongest."

Donna Karan

It happened to Donna Karan the way it did to the archetypical understudy in Hollywood musicals of the thirties: she went out a nobody and came back a star. Except that she didn't go on the stage. She stayed behind the scenes, crying. For forty minutes. "I had kept all my emotions inside while I got the collection together. I had done the best I could. Suddenly when the music started I began to bawl. But as soon as it was over, I knew it had worked. By that time, everybody else was crying too."

The year was 1974, and just two months after her daughter, Gabrielle, was born. Eight days later her boss, Anne Klein, had died. It was decided that the firm would go on, with Donna Karan, Anne Klein's assistant, doing the fall collection.

"I wasn't afraid," she recalls. "After all, nobody knew anything about me. There were no preconceived notions. I could just do what I could do. It was the next collection that was the worst. Could I follow through? I really believe in slow climbing, at your own pace. But I didn't have that luxury. I was just catapulted into it."

Donna Karan managed the second collection just fine, and the Anne Klein company is as secure as it was during its founder's life. In 1977 she and her associate, Louis dell'Olio, won a Coty Award on their own. Together, they have changed the direction of the company, which in the 1960's was known for its sharply tailored sportswear designs. Anne Klein was as responsible as any other single individual for the astonishing popularity of sportswear, first among American women,

Donna with husband, Mark, and daughter, Gabby.
preceding page, Donna and Louis the night they received
the Coty Award.

and then among the fashionable women
all over the world. Blazers, trench coats
and pants cut like men's trousers were among
the Klein specialities.

Recently the mood has softened. Blazers,
when they are done, are made without linings. Skirts are soft and move fluidly. Stiffen-
ing has disappeared. "Not only are we changing, but fashion is changing," Donna observes.
"The most important thing today is that
clothes move with the body. They can be tailored, but they have to move. As a female, I ap-

prove of this. I always think of myself and my
needs when I design. I drape the clothes on
myself as well as on models, and I feel this is
the direction. If Anne were alive today, God
knows what she would be doing, but she
would be changing with the times, because
that's what fashion is all about. And to me,
the times are saying, 'Feminine, soft, moving
with the body.'"

The Anne Klein collections today are a col-
laborative effort between Donna Karan and
Louis dell'Olio. "We battle ideas together,
like Anne and I did. We look at fabrics, and he
likes one color and I like another. He ex-
poses me to things I don't know about, and I

than me. We were a team even then. We complement each other today. I'm a yeller. Louis is very organized. We fight all the way, but we're usually happy with the end product."

Donna left Parsons in her second year to work for Anne Klein. After eight months, she was fired because, she admits, she was "immature." She thought about going back to school but went to work for designer Patti Cappalli instead. It was on a trip to Europe with her that "I saw my whole life ahead of me as a mad woman designer and I decided I had to have something else. Mark—I met him when I was fifteen years old on a blind date in Miami—came to the airport when I got home. We were married three days later."

When she left Patti Cappalli, there were many job offers. "Everybody wanted to put me in business because I had worked for Anne Klein and she was the first with sportswear, but I thought, Why should I rush into failure? So I called up Annie and I asked if I could come back. 'I've grown up a little bit,' I told her. The second time it stuck."

In the first years of her marriage Donna commuted from Seventh Avenue to her house in Lawrence, Long Island. Now she's moved to the city, where she hopes to be able to spend more time with her daughter. "We sketch together. If you ask her 'What does Mommy do?' she says, 'Mommy draws' or 'She colors.' I think she has artistic talent, but I don't care what she does when she grows up, as long as she's happy. Let her be a model or a doctor, let her stay home. Living is fulfilling your own desire."

Donna Karan doesn't think she could ever stay home "because I have to be involved—if I could accomplish as much as I do at work, it might be possible, but I can't imagine that." There might be a brother or sister for Gabby, however. She's thinking about that. And if there is, Louis is there to mind the store for the few minutes she might have to be away.

do the same to him. I guess I see Louis more than any other human being, including my husband." (Mark Karan is a retailer with two shops in Brooklyn and Long Island named Gabby after their daughter—he carries quality fashion merchandise, including Anne Klein.)

The collaboration between Donna and Louis began at the Parsons School of Design, "where we were the only students who didn't live in Manhattan," she recalls. "I lived in Woodmere and he lived in Elmont—both on Long Island—and we were always at each other's houses. I could drape better than he could and he could sketch better

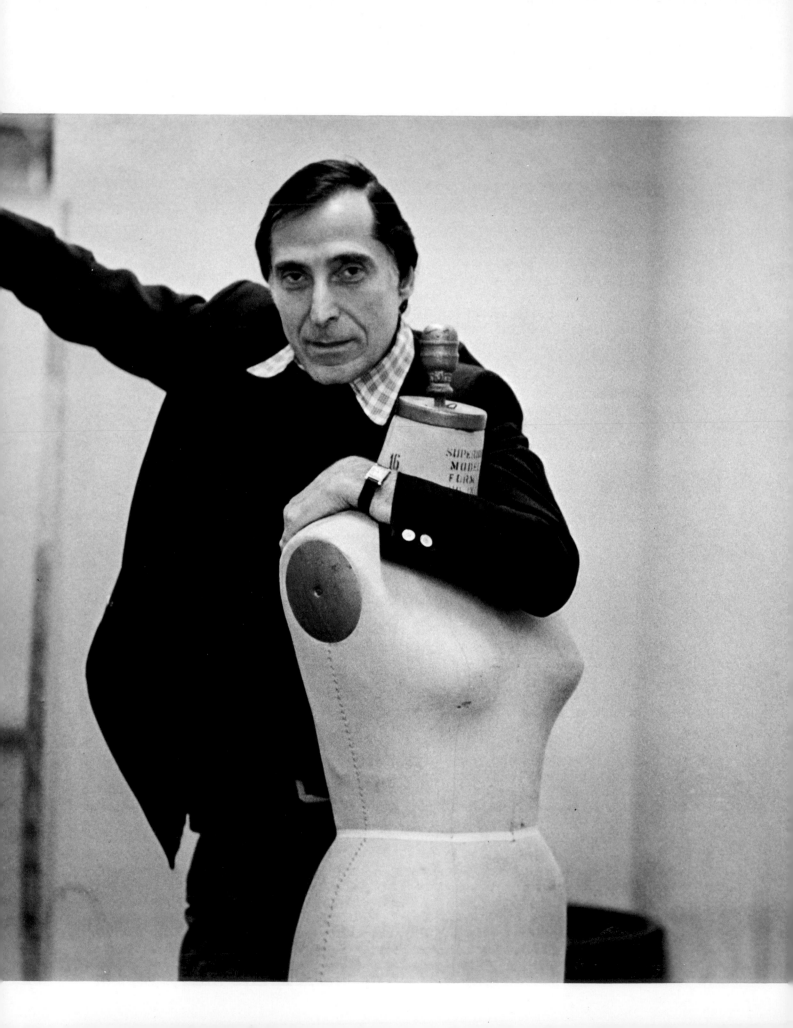

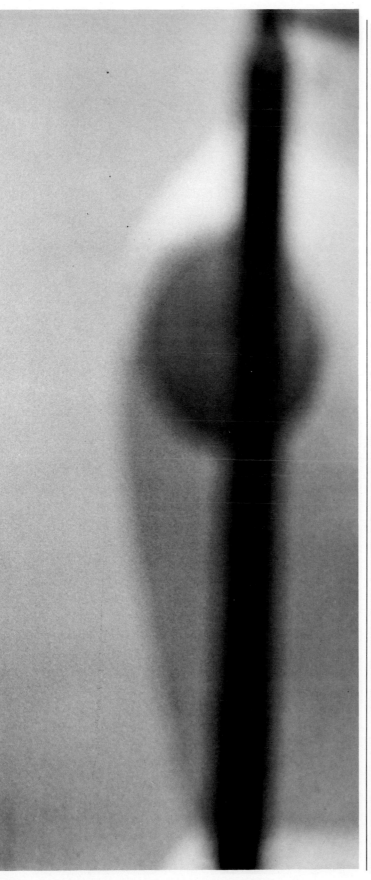

Kasper

"When I saw them coming down the runway, they looked so beautiful, I was so pleased with them. They were all my children." Herbert Kasper was talking about the showing of one of his collections to an audience of fashion reporters and store buyers. He was happy about his clothes. These days he's happy about his work.

Twenty-one years after receiving his first Coty Award, he was elected to fashion's Hall of Fame in 1976. The following year he was chosen president of the Council of Fashion Designers of America, an organization of leading personalities on Seventh Avenue. All this does not mean his growth has stopped. Kasper feels his best work is just beginning, and his recent collections indicate that he's right.

He has long been known as a respectable craftsman. After more than twenty years of respectable activity, he is apparently entering his most creative phase. Perhaps the key to his accomplishment is that he cares about his work; he cares about women enjoying his clothes. "It's not just a question of selling a dress. I want the woman who buys it to enjoy it and come back for more. I want her to feel and look good in it. That is part of the satisfaction."

His satisfied customers include Barbara Walters, whom he met the year before his first Coty Award when she was a researcher on the Tex and Jinx breakfast show. He has clothed her on her way up. "She's a very feminine woman," he says. "Because of her television work, she loves and needs color in her clothes. Anything she buys is geared to her work."

He advises Miss Walters, as he does any woman he meets during his appearances at stores, to acquire a wardrobe in which the individual pieces all work together: "People should think of what they already own and what they need. They should never buy anything that doesn't work with what they have. Years ago, when I was working in Paris, I watched women buy custom-made clothes. They spent a lot of money on clothes, but they went about it like an accountant. They figured out they would be two weeks on the Riviera, a month in Brazil, a month in Paris,

137

and they bought the clothes they needed for each place.

"From the time I started designing, I thought about clothes working together. It was partly a result of my observations in Paris and partly instinct. If I made a coat, I made a few dresses it could be worn with and maybe a skirt and shirt. This idea has developed into the sportswear concept and it's a way of life today."

Besides Barbara Walters, Kasper's fans include Lynda Bird Johnson, who frequently visited his showroom on Seventh Avenue, and Julie Nixon, when her father was in the White House. Recently he acquired the business of the whole Carter family—Rosalyn and her three daughters-in-law. Another new fan is Joanne Carson, who says, "His clothes are so feminine, sexy really. He's got a totally female concept. For a traveler like myself, it's so easy to get myself together. I don't really have to think about it. He does the thinking for me."

Johnny Carson's wife, like Miss Walters, has adopted Kasper's concept of acquiring clothes that work together and also work for their lives. "It's easy to get carried away by a particular style or a particular color that looks appealing but doesn't relate to anything," the designer says. "I've done it myself. I'd go to Venice for a week and buy a load of garish clothes that I never could wear anyplace else ever."

Kasper was born in New York, attended De Witt Clinton High School in the Bronx and then enrolled at New York University, where he majored in English and advertising. He was drafted just after World War II ended and was stationed in Germany as part of the army of occupation. Soon he ended up as a chorus boy and toured Europe in shows for soldiers put on by Special Services. He even did some costumes for the shows.

Kasper is known as one of the best social dancers on Seventh Avenue and few people realize he had some semiprofessional training. He returned to New York University after his Army stint and then went to Parsons School of Design. "I had wanted to be a designer since I was ten years old, but it's hard to tell the other kids when they want to be robbers or cops," he says.

After Parsons, he decided to go to Paris, which was obligatory for would-be designers in those postwar days. He went to the

Chambre Syndicale's school and sold sketches to French magazines like *Elle*. Before he left for Europe, he had met a milliner, who was half of the John Frederics design team, and who offered him a job. He declined but said he would send him sketches from abroad. "I didn't do anything for a year," he recalls, "because I didn't know how to draw a hat on the head. But he made a fuss and said I was lazy, so I sat down with old costume books, traced hats and got the hang of it."

When he returned to New York after two years, he went to work for Mr. Fred, as the milliner was called. Soon he left for a job designing dresses for a company called Penart.

Kasper and long-time friend Barbara Walters.

Lord & Taylor, which had taken the initiative in promoting American designers, said they wanted to feature his work. "That's where the one name started—they thought it sounded slick," the designer recalls. He was known for a while as Kasper of Penart, and then he moved to another company, Arnold & Fox. For making modestly priced clothes look like expensive ones, he received the Coty Award in 1955. Nine years later he moved to Joan Leslie, where he has remained ever since. His specialty was dresses, but seeing the handwriting on the wall, he persuaded the company to add a sportswear business a few years ago. J.L. Sport has become a thriving company as well. Often he designs a coat for Joan Leslie dresses that can work equally well with his separates for J.L. Sport. It's part of his basic theme: clothes should go together.

Kasper used to be a great man about town and he still goes out quite a bit. It's necessary to see how people live, he says, but he tries to exercise restraint: "I'm at work at eight a.m. and sometimes I don't leave until eight p.m. It's a six-day-a-week business. I work too hard to be able to go out every night."

Calvin Klein

Designers, like baseball players, sometimes achieve movie-star status. Their pictures appear in the papers. They are recognized in restaurants. Total strangers come up in the street and call them by their first name.

Calvin Klein is one of these stars. A bit too clean-cut and carefully dressed to pass as a rock singer, he nevertheless has a similar charisma. He's tall, lean and boyish-looking. Though now into his thirties, he's taken for nineteen. Though he knows what he wants, he's never pushy about himself. That slight hesitancy, in fact, is part of the charm.

Celebrity status is a by-product of what Calvin Klein wanted "ever since I was old enough to push a pencil." He decided very early in life that he wanted to be a fashion designer, but more than that, that he wanted to own his own business.

Things worked out, but not in a haphazard way. His life followed a certain course.

From the beginning he was drawn to tailored clothes because that was the kind of thing his mother wore. "She never was the frilly type," he recalls. "She had tailored coats and suits by Ben Zuckerman, George Carmel, Seymour Fox. I grew up around that kind of thing and that's what I was interested in at the beginning."

He was inspired by a teacher he had at the High School of Industrial Art (now the High School of Art and Design). He went on to the Fashion Institute of Technology, where he is now on the board of directors. And all the time he was analyzing the fashion business and his potential place in it.

He went to work as a coat designer for Dan Millstein. He earned $75 a week, and then

141

when he got married he was raised to $100. Less than ten years later he moved his own business into the same floor of the building. He left for another house making junior-size coats and suits which sold for $19 at wholesale. When his boss asked why he couldn't make as good a style as one he had been copying for years, he quit.

His friend Barry Schwartz, who was running a supermarket in Harlem, took $2,000 out of his cash register so the designer could prepare a collection. Klein brought the three dresses and six coats to Mildred Custin, then the president of Bonwit Teller, and she ordered them for the store. When they arrived in stock, they began to sell immediately.

Why coats? It wasn't only that Klein understood tailored clothes because his mother wore them. It was that he analyzed the fashion business and found that coats were the least interesting, least inventive of the categories of clothes. So he designed some that were simple enough but captured the spirit of the day.

Having established himself in 1967 as a coat designer, he saw other things happening in fashion. Sportswear was the growing field as women turned away from dresses to the casual convenience of skirts and pants or sweaters and skirts. He designed a sportswear collection and, to emphasize the change, made no coats for a season. The gamble paid off. Business increased at a rapid rate.

In recent seasons he saw the interest in sharply tailored sports clothes turning to something softer. He relaxed the styling and the construction. He made linen blouses which he put together with flannel skirts.

With his business approaching a sales volume of $25 million a year, he does not intend making it much bigger. He's looking for other outlets. A cosmetics line is being planned; so are men's clothes.

As soon as Calvin Klein went into business, Barry Schwartz closed his supermar-

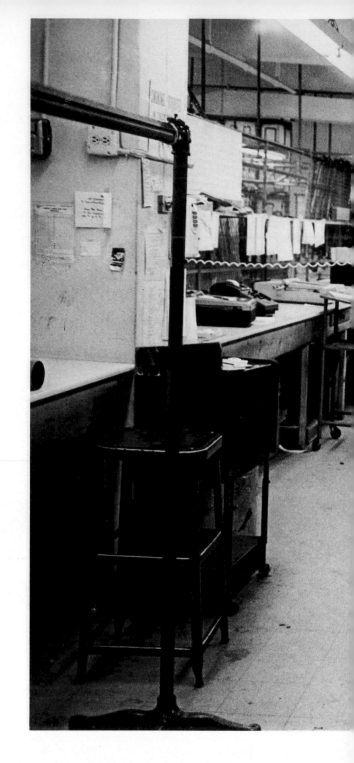

Calvin and Diana Vreeland.

ket and joined him. "The reason for my success has got to be Barry," he says. "He is absolutely brilliant about running a business. If something happened to him I would close it. There is no one else I could work with. I make the five-year plans, Barry sees that we get there."

The two have been friends since childhood. Klein, who is divorced, has a daughter, Marci. He worries about her, as any other doting father. She's an incredibly sensitive child, he says, sensitive to people. She's ten years old now and he's already concerned about what kind of woman she will grow up to be.

Unpretentious about his work, he has always said, "I make clothes people like to wear." He has never gone in for histrionics. When pressed further, he will admit that he worked hard and was disciplined. Now he says he can play hard too. "I've surrounded myself with key people who are extensions of myself. They know what I want almost as well as I do myself. I used to feel guilty when I stayed away from the business. Now I don't feel so guilty any more."

He bought a house on Fire Island, where he had rented one for years, and another in Con-

necticut. He drives a Rolls-Royce. He has an apartment on the East River which gives him a panoramic view of New York.

About fashion he says, "It's easier to get to the top than to stay there. People are hungry for anything that is good and will encourage you on the way up. To be consistent is the trick." His clothes are consistent. They are never way out. Except for a few breaks with tradition, one season's collection grows out of the one before.

"The American woman has had enough gimmicky, overdesigned clothes," he says "Now she is interested in beautiful fabrics, subtle colors and simpler things. It's not easy to design or to make simple clothes, but that's what one has to do today. Besides, it's what I like to do."

Calvin Klein has attracted such fans as Jacqueline Onassis, Liv Ullmann, Pat Buckley, Susan Brinkley, Lauren Hutton and Nancy Reagan, but he insists he hasn't made his success on snob appeal. He wants many women to enjoy his clothes, to feel serene and comfortable in them: "I don't like a lot of heaviness and bulk. I like clothes that slide when the body moves. They have to be easy and free, not stiff. When clothes are simple and beautiful, they permit the sense of the woman wearing them to come through."

145

Kenneth Jay Lane

When Kenneth Jay Lane got his first job in New York in the art department of *Vogue* magazine, he would startle Jessica Daves, the editor, by turning up for lunch at Michael's Pub, then the chic place to eat, at a table near hers—and remaining after she had gone back to work.

"I would go to the office in my English suits—suit, really—bowler hat and Sulka gloves. My life style was a little unsettling. And it wasn't easy to accomplish on fifty dollars a week."

While his name appears on many things, his mainstay is jewelry designing. Like Coco Chanel in the 1920's, he made costume jewelry fashionable in the 1960's—among women who could afford the real thing: "It became the fashionable thing for visitors from Europe to pick up a piece of Kenny Lane jewelry when they were in this country. Princess Margaret had some, so did the Duchess of Windsor. I was lucky. It became a craze."

His first big success was rhinestone jewelry: "They were pasting rhinestones on shoes and they didn't come off, so I thought it should be done in jewelry. Bonwit Teller bought some and sold them out, and before long I was selling every store on Fifth Avenue." He was working as a shoe designer when he got the idea for the jewelry. Later he decided to cover bracelets with cobraskin. (The company that did the work for him covered the heels of shoes with snakeskin.) The cobra bracelets also became a fad.

Kenneth Jay Lane was born in Detroit, where his father was a supplier of automobile parts. At the University of Michigan he

146

met Frank O'Hara, a graduate student, who introduced him to the world of art and literature in New York. One weekend in New York, he met Carrie Donovan, who took him to a party where he met Hubert de Givenchy, the French couturier, and Norman Norell, and he liked their life style.

It was a turning point: "It was the first time I thought about the fashion world—I had planned to be an art director. Now I decided I would be the art director of *Vogue* or *Harper's Bazaar*."

After graduating from the Rhode Island School of Design, he did get the job at *Vogue*, which led to other contacts with fashion people and to designing shoes for Delman.

But jewelry is his main interest, and he doesn't think it will ever go out of style: "Women are always decorating themselves. We've had hatless periods—in the seventeenth and early eighteenth century, for example, but through all of history we've never had a time when women didn't adorn themselves. There were flash fads in the 1960's and that doesn't happen any more because women are too busy expressing themselves individually. But that doesn't mean that jewelry is out. There isn't any one style, there are many styles, just as there are in clothes. That is simply the spirit of the day."

Ralph Lauren

Barbra Streisand and Frank Sinatra have called him up for clothes. Journalist Sally Quinn and consumer advocate Betty Furness also find that his classic designs fit in with their life styles. So do any number of people who have a sense of the enduring along with a feeling for what is contemporary. Ralph Lauren's business, in less than ten years, is running at the rate of about $12 million a year for his men's clothes, $8 million for his women's styles. Reversing the usual trend, he began with men's clothes, then entered the women's field. Starting with Pierre Cardin and Yves Saint Laurent in Paris, and Bill Blass, Geoffrey Beene and John Weitz in this country, the pattern has been that a designer makes his mark in the women's field before tackling the men's area.

With Ralph Lauren, the success story started with a tie—a wide tie. It was part of the "peacock revolution" of the 1960's, when formerly crew-cut types began growing sideburns, wearing chains around their necks and giving up their Brooks Brothers gray-flannel suits. Some more adventurous men adopted the Edwardian-dandy look imported from Europe and publicized by the Beatles, with its long, skinny jackets and tight, belled trousers. Women expressed their sense of social change by adopting the mini skirt. Men needed a symbol too. For them, it was a change in the width of their tie. Ralph Lauren saw the change coming and helped it along.

Born and raised in the Bronx, he studied business at the College of the City of New York—and hated it. He worked as a salesman at Brooks Brothers and learned all about the gray-flannel suit. A job with a tie company in Boston followed. He left it to set up his own business. He called the company Polo for the connotations of class carried by the rich man's sport of the 1920's. The ties were four to five inches wide, as compared with the usual three inches, and they caught on immediately.

Since the wider ties made a bigger knot, they required a bigger shirt collar to look their best. That in turn required a jacket with wider lapels. Within a year and a half Ralph Lauren was making shirts and then suits.

"It couldn't happen today," he says. "So much is happening in fashion, the tie is only a small part of what's going on. You couldn't start a business based on a change in the shape of a tie. But then men weren't used to having too much happen in the style of their clothes. The tie was a big change, but not so bizarre that men couldn't accept it."

Having established his look for men—his suits were more shaped than the old gray-flannel sack suit but less stiff than the European suits—he began thinking about women's clothes. His wife, Ricky, had a good deal to do with how he thought women should look. He met her at an eye doctor's, where she worked afternoons while she attended Hunter College. Six months later, just before she graduated, they were married.

Ricky Lauren is small and shapely, with shiny brown hair. To Ralph, "she looked sexy in well-fitted casual clothes. I didn't think it was necessary for a woman to dress like a vamp, like Jean Harlow or Marilyn Monroe, to look attractive. Being comfortable is more important than being slinky."

Just as he started his men's business with a tie, he started his women's collection with shirts. They resembled men's shirts, but they were cut for a woman's body. After the shirts

Bob Mackie

Bob Mackie has the widest exposure of any fashion designer: his specialty is television. "If you get into fifty million homes, a lot of people see your work," he says. "When I started putting Cher into halter dresses and clingy jerseys, other women started to turn up in them all over the country, so you knew they were watching.

"Cher doesn't care how crazy the things are you put on her—she's never uncomfortable. She wears everything like a T-shirt and a pair of jeans. She's never intimidated by clothes and that's why she wears them so well.

"Carol Burnett is another story. She's not comfortable in sexy clothes. She's five feet seven and she wears a size eight, so there's no question she could wear them, but she doesn't think of herself as that kind of woman. So I keep her clothes easy and loose. I put pockets on each side so she can stick her hands into them and look gracious, like the woman next door—if she were a television star.

"That's really the secret of dressing—you have to wear what you feel comfortable in. It's true of women in private life as well as of entertainers. If you feel comfortable you're going to be relaxed and have a good time. If you feel funny you're lost."

"Television is "like an x-ray," he says. "It shows all. So the clothes have to be well made. Fitting is important. Inner construction is important. They may only be on the screen for five minutes, but they have to be perfect."

Movies pose the same problem, but they're a little different. "If an actress wears the same dress all the way through the picture, you can bet she has more than one. Sometimes the neckline is changed a little bit for close-ups. Sometimes the hem is changed for long shots."

He's done some film work too: Diana Ross's clothes in *Lady Sings the Blues*—with his partner, Ray Aghayan—Barbra Streisand's in *Funny Lady*, and "housedresses, skirts and blouses" for Debbie Reynolds in *Divorce American Style*. In fact, it was the film *American in Paris*, with clothes by Irene Sharaff, that helped focus him on fashion design as a career. "I saw it ten or twelve times. I was entranced by the magic of what happens on the screen. It was the first time I ever thought about who did the costumes."

Mackie was born in Los Angeles, where he still lives. His father worked for a bank, and there was no family connection with anything theatrical. "I might as well have lived in Kansas City," he remarks. But after *American in Paris*, he went to Pasadena City College to study art, and then to art school in

154

Bob and Carol Burnett.

Los Angeles where he could study fashion design.

"In school, you were pushed into ready-to-wear, and I kept fighting it. Afterwards, I got some offers for jobs in the garment industry out here, and I resisted them. So I starved. Finally, somebody got sick and I began working for Jean Louis, the movie designer, as a sketch artist. The film was *Something's Got to Give*, the Marilyn Monroe picture that was never finished. But it was a beginning, and I shuttled between Jean Louis and Edith Head as an assistant.

"I was very much in the back room. Then the film studios began closing down in the 1960's and there wasn't much hope that somebody's assistant could find work. I began thinking about television. The first job I got was assisting Ray Aghayan on the Judy Garland show. It lasted twenty-six weeks, and then I began getting calls for jobs Ray couldn't handle."

One of Mackie's favorites was *The Wonderful World of Burlesque* "when I dressed women like Carol Channing, Lucille Ball, Lee Remick and Cyd Charisse as burlesque queens—it was great fun." He did the clothes for the King Family shows, which included

"mommies, daddies, grannies and children," and, for the past ten years, has designed clothes for the Carol Burnett show. "She's so terrific and so nice—I've never had an argument with her," he says.

He met Cher years ago when she was a guest on the Carol Burnett show. "She said someday she would come to me and I would make her something with beads, and one day she did come knocking on my door. I wanted to go on vacation at the time, but I couldn't turn her down. It was the show she and Sonny were doing as a summer replacement and we expected it to last only thirteen weeks. Well, you know what happened."

Mackie doesn't feel as violent about doing ready-to-wear today as he did when he was starting out. He designs bathing suits for Cole of California, is planning to do loungewear, and for a time he and Aghayan designed a dress collection. "It was mainly evening clothes with an ultra-glamour feeling," he recalls. "We tried to do it at the same time we were doing theater things, and it was just sort of breaking even, so we dropped it after a couple of years. But I don't think of ready-to-wear as a backbreaking chore the way I did when I was younger. Of course, I don't have to do the boring things I was asked to do when I was just starting out."

Mary McFadden

She was brought up on her father's cotton plantation in Memphis until she was ten. After her father's death her mother moved her and her two brothers back to the family home in Westbury, Long Island. She attended Foxcroft, a school in Middleburg, Virginia, and, after graduation, spent a year in Paris. She studied at the Traphagen School of Design, Columbia University and the New School for Social Research before she married and moved to South Africa with her husband.

During her time in Africa she founded a sculpture workshop in Rhodesia and traveled all over that continent and Asia examining ancient and modern art. "A study of classical forms keeps style pure and alive," she says. "It is important to have a huge knowledge of ancient civilizations to understand proportion. I draw upon my background constantly in the production of my jewelry as well as my fabrics."

In her prints, especially, she seeks to "revitalize the past in terms of modern technology, to produce through our screening techniques the aura of ancient robes." Yes, she will admit, her clothes are art. But, she insists, "I consider them very wearable."

When she brought those first three dresses to Bendel's, she thought it was a one-shot deal. Two months later, "I realized I would be in this business." Today she is committed to it. She also believes she has to have a unique product if she is to stay in it: "There is no point in coming to Seventh Avenue and doing copies of Bill Blass. You have to present something that isn't available any place else."

Besides dresses, what Mary McFadden is selling is style. That is a rare commodity anywhere and she has cornered the market on a particular exotic variety. There are enough people who appreciate it to bring her annual sales volume to $3 million for dresses, an extra million for jewelry. Women in a McFadden dress don't look like any other women, except perhaps the other McFadden fans. They all belong to an exclusive club.

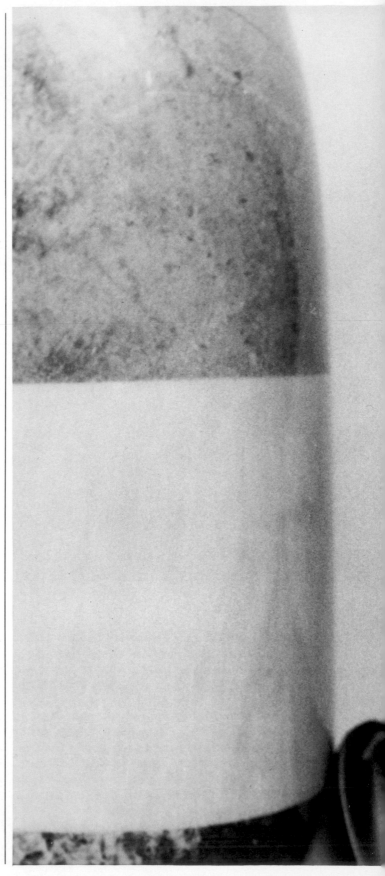

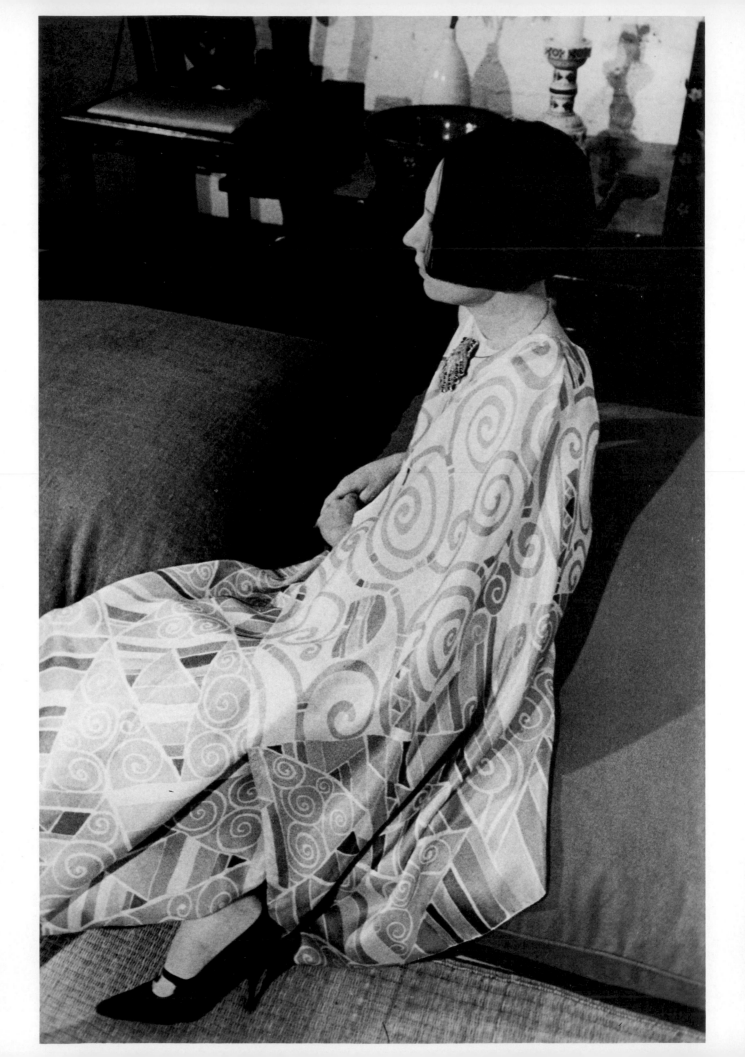

It's not the usual dress manufacturer's showroom. Beads are strung along one wall to make a collage. Paper lanterns hang from the ceilings. Vases, masks and wood sculptures from Africa decorate the vast loft area.

She's not the usual dress manufacturer. Mary McFadden is reed-slim with jet-black hair, enormous eyes and chalk-white skin. She is a woman of enormous personal style, an original.

Her clothes also are original, based on simple shapes derived from ancient peasant costumes in the Near and Far East. They're made of finely pleated fabrics and filmy silks or quilting, and they're often exotic prints derived from a detail on an African mask or an Indian sandal. They're shown with, and often worn with, jewelry of hand-beaten brass dipped in 18-karat gold. The jewelry is based on archaic symbols of many ancient civilizations. The jewelry adds an extra dimension to the clothes, but it is the fabric that is most important, she believes.

"We're really in the fabric business, the fabric sells the goods," says Mary McFadden, sounding for a moment like a dress manufacturer. After they are used for dresses, the prints are adapted for upholstery and wallpaper, which she does for the Raintree division of Kirk-Brummel, or the table coverings she designs for Leacock.

The business began in 1973, when she brought three dresses she had designed for herself to Geraldine Stutz, the president of Henri Bendel, who encouraged her to produce them. They were austere tunic-like designs that floated around the body.

The McFadden designs are never complicated, but on the right woman they produce a startling, highly individual effect. Jacqueline Onassis was the right woman the night the exhibit of Russian costumes opened at the Metropolitan Museum of Art. In the vast expanse of the museum's Great Hall the women who stood out were not those in simple silk crepe or chiffon dresses. They were the ones in the bouffant taffeta ball gowns made by or inspired by Yves Saint Laurent in Paris. Except for Mrs. Onassis. She stood in the re-

ceiving line in a pleated white strapless column by Mary McFadden and made the more elaborately gowned women look overdressed. She proved one of McFadden's basic points: that austerely simple classic cuts make a woman look more beautiful.

At almost any big social event in New York it is easy to spot one or, more frequently, a number of Mary McFadden designs on women who care about clothes. They include the high priestess of fashion, Diana Vreeland, Lee Radziwill, Ethel Kennedy, Mrs. William S. Paley, Mrs. Gardner Cowles, Mrs. Samuel I. Newhouse and Evelyn Lauder. "They've been called an elitist group, but I like to think of them as an artistic group," says the designer. She thinks of her clothes as an art form. Indeed, her interest in art preceded her involvement in clothes.

161

Anthony Muto

Anthony Muto has spent a lifetime making clothes. Expensive ones and cheap ones. Sophisticated clothes and wide-eyed innocent clothes. At the moment he is concerned with how women dress at night. In his collection for Marita, which is modestly priced, he has introduced ideas usually found in expensive clothes or in sportswear. There are halter or strapless tops which can be alternated with short skirts or floor-length ones. Pants can be substituted, jackets or shawls added.

Knowledgeable women have been dressing like this for a long time. Muto is making it possible for everyone. By adapting the concept of separates—or "tops and bottoms," as he puts it—to evening clothes, he makes it possible for a woman to acquire as versatile a wardrobe at night as the sweaters and skirts she assembles for day. The clothes last longer and they serve more purposes.

It's no longer a question of sinking a lot of money into a dress that's going to be worn to a wedding or a special party and worrying about when it can be used again. The separate pieces can be assembled differently on different occasions. They can be put together with other pieces in a wardrobe to change their mood further. Best of all, they can be purchased to fit properly in the beginning: if a woman happens to have a size-ten top and a size-twelve bottom, she doesn't have to worry about alterations—she can buy two different sizes.

"Ready-to-wear is the American dream," he says. "The whole idea of walking into a store and walking out with something that fits is an American concept. And I think it is wonderful to give someone a variety of choices. All the work has to be done by the designer. Then the woman simply selects what suits her.

"I'm interested in making clothes that look like 'this season' but don't go out of style next season. I wasn't raised in the throw-away tradition: I think things should last."

He was raised in Chicago, where his grandfather was a tailor and his mother always sewed. He went to art school from the age of twelve, and when he graduated from

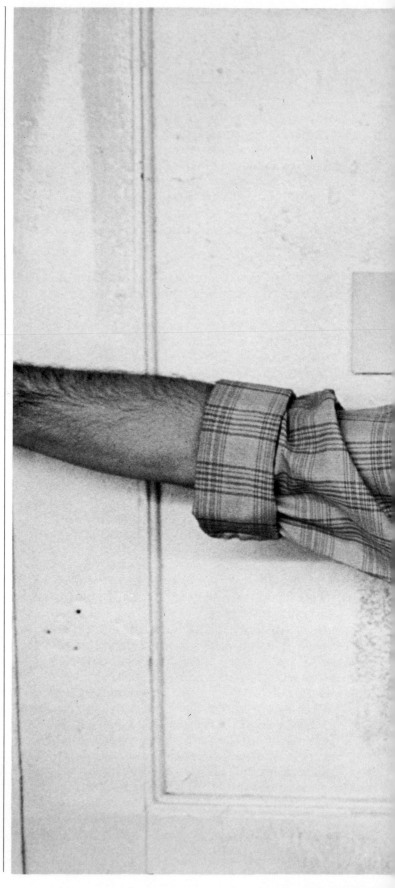

high school, he won an art scholarship. Later he was asked to return to the same art school to teach sketching, draping and pattern making. He worked at various companies in Chicago, made wedding dresses for friends, and then with his wife, LaVerne, toured Europe.

Muto was making junior dresses for Arkay when he scored his first big success. His innovations, for juniors, included kite-shaped dresses, suede dresses and doing small sizes—four first and then two. Later he designed expensive dresses for mature women and thought of designing men's clothes. In 1971 he settled in at Marita and started re-

working the evening fashion scene. Three years ago the Mutos were divorced, but he still maintains close contact with his three teenage children.

The designer's job is to make clothes that look right, but he insists that it is up to the customer to take care of them properly. When he travels with his collections to the stores, he is apt to lecture women on how to hang their clothes rather than advise them on what to buy. "It's an outrage to throw things on the floor or a chair—they should be hung on a hanger," he says. Pants should be hung on clips from the hem. When they hang, wrinkles have a chance to smooth out, so

Paul Bridgewater and Anthony in Zouave pants at the Metropolitan Museum.

they don't leave marks. Coats should be held on wide hangers so they are balanced properly—buy padded hangers for the purpose, he advises.

Most people do not know how to press well, and he recommends the steam-in-the-bathroom technique to avoid manual work with an iron. That simply involves hanging the garment in the bathroom and turning on the hot water in the shower.

For traveling, he recommends packing everything in plastic bags, and he says everyone should use shoetrees—they will make shoes last longer.

Belt loops should usually be removed from a dress or jacket. They are put there to make sure the belt doesn't disappear from the dress, but they are essentially unsightly and, besides, belts should be worn at the woman's own waistline, not where the loops are placed.

Muto tries to supply scarves with most of his clothes so that a woman can tie them in her own way to individualize the outfit.

But beyond all this, the "most important accessory" is the spirit with which a woman wears her clothes: "If she feels alive, she will look vital."

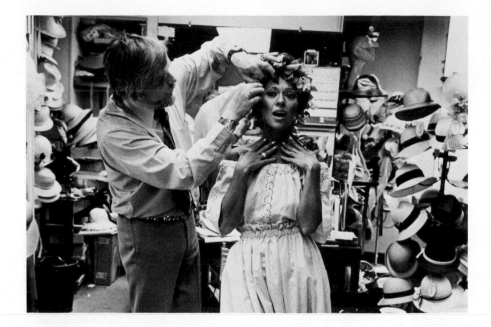

Frank Olive

"A hat is basically a prop," says Frank Olive. "As in the theater, it creates a scene, it sets a mood. It gives you a moment of joy, mystery, fantasy." He feels a hat is more personal and revealing than any other item of clothing a woman chooses to wear. To him, "It's the most private statement she can make. It tells her inner soul."

This playful, avuncular, dreamy sort of man, makes hats. Once there were a lot of milliners: Lilly Daché, Emme, Sally Victor, Walter Florell, Laddie Northridge, John Frederics and, toward the end of the era, Halston and Adolfo. Once a hat was the most important thing about a woman's costume; she went out and bought herself a new one if she was depressed. But then hair became more important than what you put over it. The hairdresser replaced the milliner in the fashionable woman's affection. The bouffant beehive in the early 1960's provided the *coup de grâce*: there was nothing you could put over it but the pillbox Jacqueline Kennedy made famous.

Halston and Adolfo went on to find fame as

Frank and Rita Moreno.

dress designers. Frank Olive's World makes dresses too, but hats are its focal point. The designer travels around the country, to stores such as I. Magnin on the West Coast, Neiman-Marcus in Texas, and Saks Fifth Avenue in Florida, to bring his romance of hats to the customers. There he still finds small groups of women who understand the magic: "She comes in with her boyfriend or her husband, sometimes she brings her daughter; she wants that touch of mystery a hat can provide. There is nothing more incredible than watching a young girl's face as she puts on her first hat and looks at herself in the mirror—sometimes she can't believe what she sees. She doesn't recognize the face that stares back at her. She has been transformed. She goes out happy."

Frank Olive designs hats which make the transformation easier, and which go with contemporary clothes. He'll make a big-brimmed hat with a round crown to be worn over a scarf and with a wreath of flowers around the crown. Each part can be worn separately. He'll taper some of the big brims at the sides so a smaller woman can wear them and not be overpowered. And he'll make crocheted caps in many colors with flowers at the edge which young girls

Frank and a customer at Saks Fifth Avenue.

particularly understand.

He was born a twin in Milwaukee, Wisconsin. He and his brother, Gerald, were identical in looks, the opposite in temperament. Whereas Gerald was precise, businesslike and practical, Frank was the dreamer. When Gerald died in 1971 Frank was crushed. He met Adri, the designer, about that time and she comforted him. They remain the closest of friends.

When he was a child, his grandmother would take him to the movies. He would go home and construct his own theater, re-creating the costumes and the settings. He thought of getting into the theater in New York and tried being a sketcher on Seventh Avenue. When Norman Norell saw his sketches, he said, "Why don't you become a milliner?"

"He was a Midwesterner too," says Olive, who feels a special affinity with people from that part of the country (Adri is from Missouri). "I told him I didn't know how, and he said, 'You'll find a way.'" About a year later he did. He opened a tiny shop in Greenwich Village that had been a popcorn stand and called it La Boutique. He thinks it may well have been the first boutique in New York. The time was the early 1950's. He made scarves, blouses and hats there, "and that's how Norell's prophecy was fulfilled—I became a milliner."

Today he turns out a tailored hat as swiftly as he makes something whimsical. He is happy that people pay money for something he likes to create. He even feels hats may be coming back into favor: "Yesterday's militant woman is softer and more playful. She's not afraid of looking feminine, of dressing up. I think she may even wear gloves again."

Mollie Parnis

She makes pretty dresses for women who are more concerned with showing off a graceful neck or waistline than they are with keeping up with the latest vagaries of fashion. She is never the first to raise or lower hemlines or to change the shape of dresses, she is not known for starting trends. Yet women remember specific dresses she initiated—a lacy knit that everyone wore to work a few years back, a sequin-paved jacket that made the simplest silk dress sparkle through countless evenings.

But Mollie Parnis is more than a dressmaker. Relatively late in life, after her husband died, she started a salon. Lyndon Johnson came to dinner. So did Henry Kissinger. Frank Sinatra and his wife, Barbara, are close friends. Walter Cronkite, Barbara Walters, Mike Wallace, Arthur Ochs (Punch) Sulzberger, the publisher of *The New York Times,* and many of his editors drop by to talk shop or trivia. Invitations to her Sunday evenings are treasured. She only invites people who interest her.

And occasionally her two lives overlap. Mrs. Cronkite and Mrs. Wallace come to her showings on Seventh Avenue. At a party a woman will want to discuss clothes. "What's in?" she will ask. The designer tries to deflect the question. "I find myself saying, 'I wish I knew.'" In off-hours she does not want to talk about fashion.

There are other things she is interested in: foreign affairs, government, the theater. When conversations on these subjects go swirling around at her dinner table, where she serves simple food and good wines, she is as fascinated as a schoolgirl.

And yet she is fascinated by her work also.

"My job has opened doors for me all over the world. It has been a privilege to know three Presidents well [she has dressed the wives of Dwight Eisenhower, Lyndon Johnson, Richard Nixon and Gerald Ford, whom she knew less well], and to have been invited to the White House often. I've been able to combine my work with my private life. If I didn't get paid, I would like to come down to Seventh Avenue every day anyway. Imagine, enjoying it and getting paid!"

It is such naive enthusiasm that makes her popular as a hostess and as a guest. There's a pragmatic side too. When a persistent acquaintance insists on advice on clothes, she tells

following page, Mollie with Mike Wallace.

her, "Buy the best you can afford, and don't discard it next year—just add something to it and build a wardrobe that will work for you."

"I was going to be a lawyer," she recalls, "but I got a summer job in a blouse house when I was attending Hunter College and I never went back to school. I thought I was a designer because I decided where to put the French knots. The young people today are so much better equipped. If I were beginning today, I don't think anyone would give me a job."

171

Elsa Peretti

She is a woman of almost awesome chic, looking as dazzling in a beat-up men's fedora as she does in a Halston ball gown. If she were in another era, she would never go out without her diamond or emerald necklace.

Jewelry designer Elsa Peretti is a contemporary woman. She lives in a small white apartment with mirrored walls, where the only furniture is a drafting table and a group of white sofas covered in cotton.

Instead of heavy diamonds or emeralds, her jewelry is apt to be a crooked silver heart on a tiny chain or a belt buckle shaped like a horseshoe. "There are people who spend three or four hundred thousand dollars for a ring," she acknowledges. "But that means you must live around your possessions. Then you must have someone to guard your ring. You can't run out and hail a taxi."

While she doesn't believe jewelry should be conspicuous, she does feel it should be made of quality materials. She works in silver, gold, ivory and, occasionally, even diamonds. The latter are hung on gold chains and can be as small as a chip or as large as a karat. Known as "diamonds by the yard," they are never overwhelming.

"Women buy their own jewelry today," she observes. This means that a secretary or a salesgirl should be able to afford her pieces. Besides being decorative in a low-keyed way, her jewelry pieces also have a tactile quality, almost like worry beads. Her bean-shaped pendant is as pleasant to touch as it is to view.

The Peretti story is, on the surface, one of those instant success stories. In less than a decade she has revolutionized attitudes toward jewelry and inspired legions of imitators. She has transformed Tiffany's jewelry section, where her things have been sold exclusively for the last few years.

But her early years were not easy. She was born in Italy to an affluent family that believed women should follow the traditional route of wife and motherhood. "My sister married and had four kids—she was the good one. I guess everything I have done was to prove I was good too, but in another way."

On her twenty-first birthday, the minute she was legally of age, she fled to Switzerland, where she taught Italian and French at the finishing school she had gone to earlier. Her mother came to Gstaad and persuaded her to return to Rome, where she attended a design school. Then she fled again, this time to Milan, where she worked in an architect's office and met Marina Schiano, who was then modeling. Marina suggested that she too take up modeling—it paid better.

"I didn't know how to do my make-up and I was terrified but I tried it," she recalls. "Marina went to America and I was too timid to do that. So I went to Spain. I had a certain success, especially in my blond wig. I went to Paris in 1967 and later to London, and finally to New York. I arrived in the middle of a garbage strike and with a black eye. I had a jealous boyfriend at the time, and he didn't want me to leave.

"Soon I met Giorgio Sant' Angelo and we became great friends. I told him I wanted to do some jewelry and he encouraged me. The first thing I did was the little bottle or bud vase and the belt. Giorgio showed them with his collection and they became a success.

"As soon as I became known for my jewelry, I began to be in demand as a model. I did both things for a while. I sold my jewelry

to Bloomingdale's through Halston, and then he introduced me to the Tiffany people and soon I was beginning to make some money."

About five years ago she bought a house in a tiny village about an hour and a half's drive from Barcelona.

"A friend, a photographer, showed me a picture and I thought I must have it. It cost two thousand dollars, and then for the same amount of money I bought another house near it, and I made a bridge between the two."

Later she bought additional buildings—mostly in ruins—and built a sauna and a swimming pool. "All the money I made from Tiffany went into my houses," she says.

What she hopes to establish there eventually is a sanctuary for artistic people, working in "total calm," away from the frenetic diversions of civilization.

How much time does she plan to spend in Spain?

"I would prefer to go frequently from New York to work there. I need the quiet. New York is where everything is happening and I need the stimulation, but I find it difficult to work—there are too many distractions. There is so much social life, it drains me. But my home in Spain is so remote, it encourages me to work. It brings me energy."

177

Oscar de la Renta

On his fortieth birthday a few years back Oscar de la Renta parried the playful condolences of his friends. "If my life were to end now," he said, "I would have no regrets. I've lived every day to the fullest and I've had a marvelous time. I've tried to be nice to the people I care about and ignore the ones I don't. I enjoy what I've done."

As a fashion designer of international reputation, he has dressed such women as Nancy Kissinger, Pat Buckley, Lee Radziwill and Babe Paley. He shares some elegant clients—Marie-Hèlene de Rothschild, Marella Agnelli—with Yves Saint Laurent and Valentino. Those designers, and Bill Blass, are among his closest friends.

At his New York apartment, decorated by

181

his wife, Françoise de Langlade, who was once fashion editor of French *Vogue*, he entertains writers, theater people, political figures ("people with a tremendous commitment to life") at small dinners once or twice a week. Weekends he relaxes in his country house in Kent, Connecticut, and whenever he can spare a few extra days he flies to his place in Santo Domingo, where he was born. "For me, it is important to go back home—I'm proud that the Dominicans are proud of me," he says.

Besides drawing a lot of his rich and powerful friends to the Caribbean island, he has become involved in good works there. Some years ago, he found, in a rural area, an Episcopal priest trying to care for forty orphaned children in the stable of an abandoned estate. He prodded the government to contribute some property and urged friends in the construction business to build proper dormitories and schoolrooms. Each year he does a fashion show to raise funds for the orphanage, which now shelters three hundred and seventy-five children and is comparable to Boys Town.

A glamorous figure himself—he has a slight stutter that surfaces occasionally which he turns into a charming asset instead of a handicap—he really seems to enjoy life. He also manages to do a prodigious amount of work. In addition to his main business of making clothes on Seventh Avenue, he designs men's clothes, shoes, furs, sheets, umbrellas and eyeglasses. Fashion has been good to him, and he's made his mark in it, turning out clothes that are usually outrageously feminine and flattering.

There is always a sharp dichotomy between his styles for day and those for evening. It is no accident. The day things are spare and practical, the evening ones touched with fantasy. "Probably because of my background, I usually have some sort of exotic accent," he admits.

His background was indeed unusual. The youngest of seven children, he was the only boy. "Though my mother was strict with me, I always got away with what I wanted," he recalls. After finishing high school in Santo Domingo, he persuaded his mother to send him to Madrid to study art. His father had always preferred that his son go into his insurance business, so when his mother died,

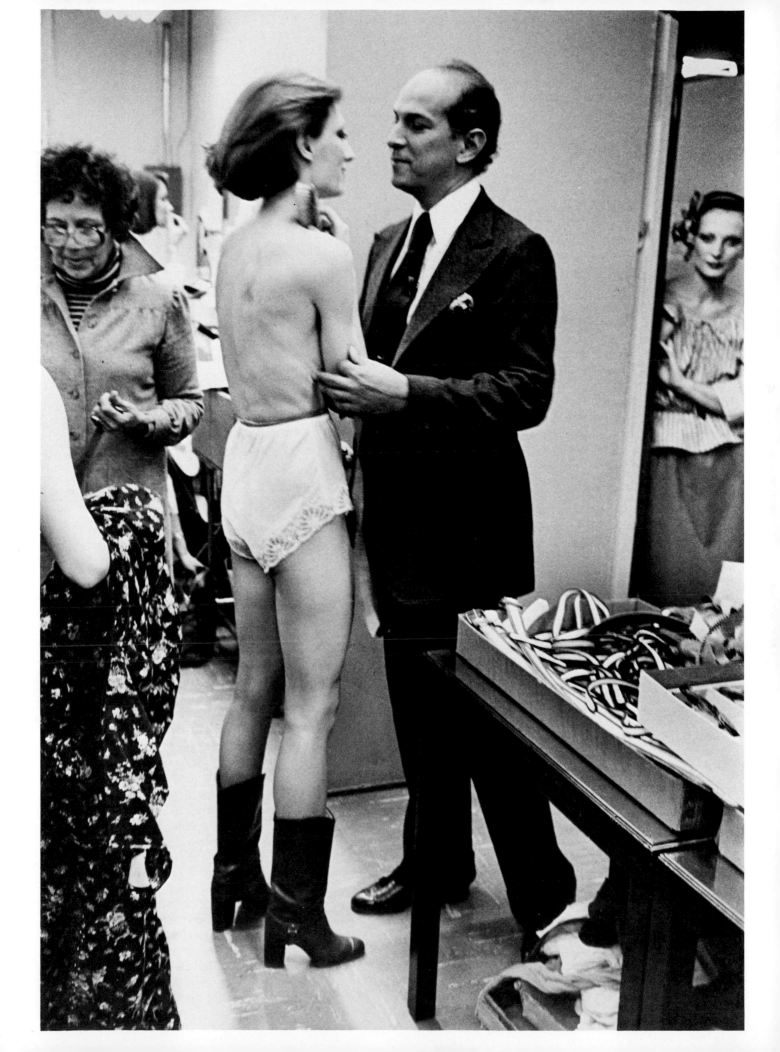

his father decided that he should come home. But the future designer could not see himself as an insurance salesman. His sisters sent him money to continue living in Spain, but he did sense pressure to start earning some money. Since he could always draw with ease, he started doing fashion illustrations for newspapers and magazines in Spain. Soon he began sketching his own ideas. A friend showed his sketches to Balenciaga, who offered him work in his Madrid house, run by his sister, Asa. Balenciaga's main establishment was in Paris, where he, along with Christian Dior, was a pillar of the couture.

"After six months I learned what fashion was all about, and I decided if I was going to stay in the field I must go to Paris," he recalls. Balenciaga thought he would be more useful if he remained in Madrid, so armed with letters of introduction from others, he set off for Paris on his own. The first day he was there he was offered a job at Dior. The second day he went to see Antonio del Castillo, who was looking for an assistant. "He loved me because I spoke Spanish, and he asked me if I could cut, drape and sew and of course I said yes. He offered me a little more money than Dior, and I said I would start in two weeks. Then I went to a fashion school and asked the

woman who ran it if she could teach me the year's course in two weeks. Of course, once I went to work for Castillo, I never had to do these things, but I knew them."

In November 1962, armed with letters to Dior, who had a manufacturing business on Seventh Avenue, and to Elizabeth Arden, who had a custom salon, he came to the United States to try his luck. He began working for Arden two months later. That's when he met some of the women who remained his fans after he moved to Seventh Avenue in his own business in 1965.

"Being well dressed hasn't much to do with having good clothes," he says. "It's a ques-tion of good balance and good common sense, a knowledge of who you are and what you are. There are many kinds of taste. The rules that apply to one person do not hold true for another. There are women who underdress and look well and women who underdress and look terrible. Gloria Guinness can pick a Mexican T-shirt in a market for two dollars and look great."

His best advice on dressing is deceptively simple: Know yourself, then dress accord-ingly. Some intuitively understand what he is talking about. They are born knowing. For others, it may take a lifetime.

Clovis Ruffin

Clovis Ruffin looks like a movie star. Tall, blond and blue-eyed, he is a folk hero to young women all over the country who adore the clothes he makes. He began with T-shirt dresses and went on to design wrap-and-tie styles which looked sexy. He is the "name designer" for women who spend $40 to $60 for their clothes. He's young enough to understand them.

Despite the sexiness of the clothes he makes, he's essentially a classicist: "My definition of bad taste is the woman who walks into a room and everybody says, 'Look at that Pucci.' A dress shouldn't precede a woman—she should come first."

Recently Ruffin has upgraded his business, adding some styles in the $100-to-$150 range, to enable him to use better fabrics and more elaborate designs. But he still believes the woman should come first.

He was born at the Air Force base in Clovis, New Mexico, which is how his mother got his first name. Until he was thirteen, he lived at Army bases all over the country. Then he moved to New York with his mother and "went to tough public schools." He attended Columbia University for a while.

"I had this hang-up," he recalls. "I wanted to do something creative, but creativity in America is not a masculine quality, so I suppressed this until I saw the movie *Blow-Up*. I decided that being a photographer was suitably creative and wouldn't embarrass my family, so I became a photographer's assistant."

He worked on the *Hair* poster and later, as a stylist, borrowed expensive women's clothes from Bill Blass and Oscar de la Renta to show with the $90 suits from the manufacturer that was his account. Then "I realized photography bored me—I didn't care about the exposures and the equipment—but I did enjoy the styling."

His first dresses were made like T-shirts in pink and baby-blue fabrics with ducks and ABC's printed on them. "I would walk around New York in a baby T-shirt with shorts and knee socks and I'd carry things in a bucket. It's a wonder I wasn't arrested," he says. But that was in the sixties, when anything went.

He made his dresses in a loft where he did the cutting and made the patterns himself, hired a few seamstresses to do the sewing and was his own shipping clerk. He sold the things to Capezio and Bloomingdale's, which bought as much as he could produce.

"I was making cheap clothes and, with cheap clothes, everything in a design sense was concentrated at the front. Everything stopped at the side seams. I thought of

clothes in the round, and I also thought of basic styles that would enable women to put the mark of their personality on them." He was negotiating with a Seventh Avenue manufacturer when he decided to present his $40 dresses on fabulous models, with outrageous accessories. "I used a lot of black models and encouraged them to dance to the hot music on the runway. There wasn't any commentary. I always thought it was silly to announce, You are now looking at a red dress." Ten minutes after the show, he signed a contract to move from his loft to Seventh Avenue. Nine months later he won a Coty Award.

Now Clovis Ruffin has convinced his family that dressmaking is a respectable calling. He is exercising his creativity, in handbags and loungewear as well as in dresses.

"Women have a lot more options in clothes than men have," he muses. "They have the ability to change their hair, to change their style. A man is always trapped with what he is."

How does he like women to look? "I'd rather see them in cotton dresses than in polyester pants suits," he says. "I'd rather see them look like themselves than like some designer's concept of how they should look." His outlook is essentially classic.

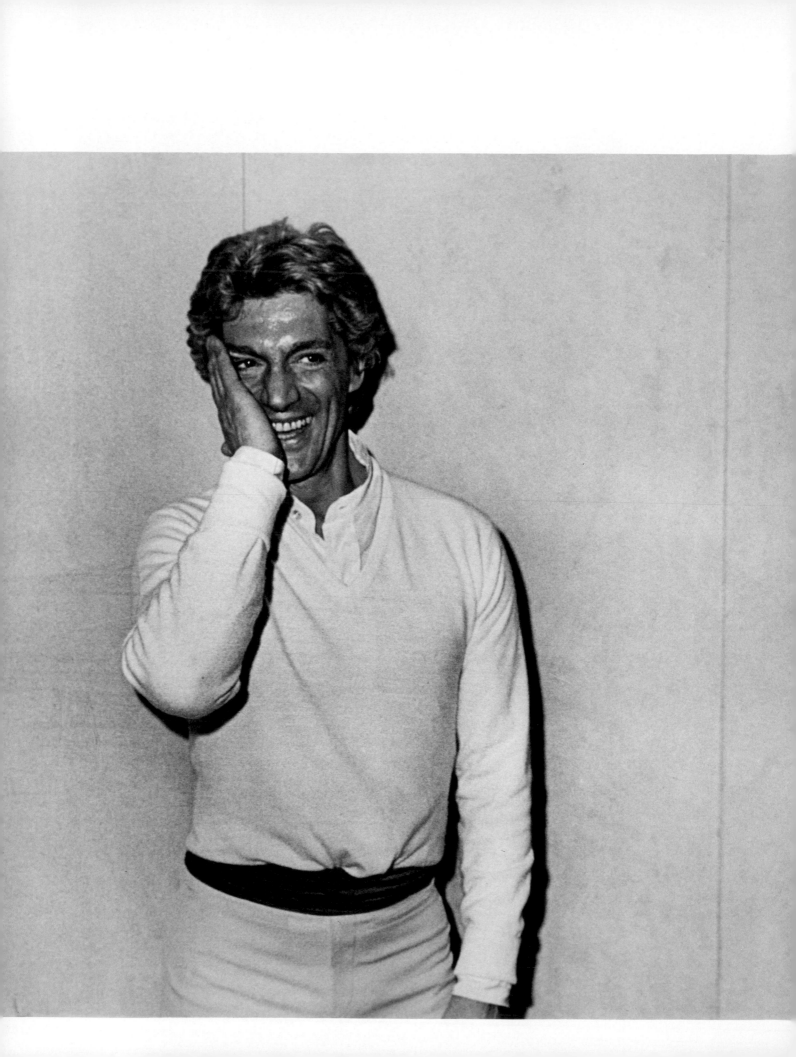

Giorgio Sant'Angelo

Giorgio di Sant'Angelo became plain Giorgio Sant'Angelo a year ago. It was part of his plan to make his life simpler. At about the same time, he moved from his old apartment in Greenwich Village to a new one on Park Avenue—just a few blocks from his workrooms on 57th Street. Before he did, he held a sale among his friends of all the gewgaws, curios and furnishings he had picked up on his travels. He painted his new apartment white and furnished it mainly with white canvas pillows on low wood bases. He removed the doors and made some white canvas screens to provide privacy when needed. Most of the furnishings he made himself. When he looked at the modern furniture available, he found it too slick, too worked over, too complicated. It did not fit into his plan to simplify his life.

"I think that's the trend in America—to live with uncluttered things, functional things," he says. "If I were an architect, I would make all apartments one room, with no walls, and let everyone living in them make their own divisions."

Actually, he was trained as an architect and industrial designer before he went into fashion and contributed to the excitement of the 1960's with his elaborately draped gypsy clothes and, later, his Indian styles.

Sant'Angelo was born in Florence and grew up in Argentina on his grandfather's farm, which was "ten hours from the nearest town." When he was seventeen, he returned to Florence with his parents and studied architecture there. He attended the Institute of Industrial Design in Barcelona, studied art at the Sorbonne, and came to this country to do animated cartoons for the Walt Disney Studios in California. Later he was working as a textile designer when he got hold of some plastic which he took home to play around with. He turned it into jewelry, which served as his entry into the fashion field. Soon after that, he began tying scarves to create his gypsy look. "American women were wearing stiff boxes with zippers up the back as dresses," he recalls. "I thought it was time for them to loosen up. Why not be gypsies?"

The Indians came later. He reasoned, Why go anywhere in the world for inspiration when we have the most fantastic culture right here? So he came up with his leathers, fringes and beaded clothes.

Early on, he met Lena Horne, who has remained his favorite customer. "She bought my plastic jewelry and she said, 'If you don't make dresses for another black woman entertainer, I will never wear anybody else's designs.' That was eleven years ago, and I still love her," he says.

There are two aspects to his business—the made-to-order styles for Miss Horne and other entertainers, such as Faye Dunaway and her husband, Peter Wolf, Bianca and Mick Jagger ("I do a lot of couples"), and the ready-to-wear that is sold in stores throughout the country. He has also branched out into such fields as bathing suits, blouses, sheets and men's clothes. His furniture designs have also been put into production by Lane and will be available to the public this spring. He has plans for china and glass designs.

Sant'Angelo has a wild, unique talent that flourished in the 1960's in a baroque sort of way. One of his first models was Marina Schiano, now a vice president of Yves Saint Laurent in New York. She told him about her "fabulous friend" living in Italy, who turned out to be Elsa Peretti, whom he introduced to Halston. Other friends from those days were Egon and Diane Von Furstenberg, and Loulou de La Falaise, who also works for Saint Laurent.

"In the beginning, none of us had a penny. We shared our food. The girls would come and fit the clothes for me at night, after their other jobs." Then came success for all of them. But Giorgio still has a dream: "Architects and fashion designers, working together in a studio, sharing their thoughts and producing their own work with a decided style. Like the Bauhaus was early in this century. That is for the future."

192

Don Sayres

Don Sayres is a tall, personable young man who epitomizes a new type of designer drawn to Seventh Avenue. He could be an art teacher—or a banker. He has always been interested in clothes—he wears them well himself—and he has definite ideas about how people should look.

"Since I was three years old, I had opinions on color, on what colors worked well on what people," he says. It was natural to base a career on it.

He likes people to look as if they were aware of fashion—not too far ahead and certainly not behind it. His clothes are definitely mainstream. When challis is in, he makes sure he shows plenty of challis clothes. When tailoring is the rage, he provides an assortment of tailored styles. "That's my function—to be plugged into what's happening," he explains, "to be there at the right time with the right trends. Fashion is always changing. I have to decide, 'Are people tired of this thing? Are they ready for that one?'"

His typical customer is obviously the woman who cares about clothes but doesn't make them her lifework. They're affordable clothes that will make her look of-the-moment but not outré.

He works for Gamut, a company formed by Consolidated Foods in 1975. ("They have me, Sara Lee cakes, Gant shirts and Electrolux vacuum cleaners," he says.) The name expresses the concept: he makes clothes he thinks all kinds of women would like to wear. "I'm not locked into a fabric or a look," he says. "If it makes sense to me that people should want it, I do it."

So he does good gray-flannel suits with soft skirts or pants sparked with bright blue sweaters or shirts for day, and with big brown taffeta skirts with petticoats and white satin blouses for evening. "What I've hit on here is, I put the pieces and the colors together for the woman who doesn't have the time to look for a skirt in one place, a shirt in another. She's able to get herself together with one purchase. That's my contribution."

Arnold Scaasi

Arnold Scaasi is often referred to as New York's last custom designer. There are, of course, other people who make clothes to order, fitting them to the individual client, making changes in the cut and the fabric to suit her taste. But Scaasi, as he is known, still makes a collection twice a year which he presents in his salon to potential customers and the press, just as Dior, Givenchy and other couture designers do in Paris. After Scaasi, it is unlikely that anyone will bother to continue the couture tradition in this country. Women prefer to buy their clothes ready-made, so they can see what they are getting. Few are willing to invest the time for the several fittings necessary, not to mention the money for all this personal attention.

Nevertheless, Scaasi's business is flourishing, because there still are a few hundred women addicted to the sybaritic pleasures of couture clothes.

In his forties, Scaasi looks much younger. He leads the same kind of life that many of his clients do, entertaining lavishly in his duplex apartment overlooking Central Park and in his weekend home in Quogue, on Long Island, where he does much of his designing.

"When you make a custom collection, there are very few rules," he says. "You don't have to worry about the store buyer understanding your clothes, or the saleswoman presenting them properly. All you have to think about is the woman wearing your dress—making her look attractive.

"I love sitting down with the customer, discussing the kind of life she leads and working out the clothes that will enhance it. Some customers can be very creative and inspiring. Barbra Streisand came to my first custom collection in a slouch hat and a poncho. She called up the next day and asked whether the bridal gown could be made in black as an evening coat. It was a fabulously creative idea and I knew this woman had something."

This was back in 1964, and Scaasi has continued to dress Streisand, along with other theatrical personalities, such as Diahann

Carroll, Arlene Francis and Dina Merrill.

Before starting his custom business, Scaasi worked on Seventh Avenue, doing extravagant styles—coats of feathers or elaborate creations in satin. He still specializes in dramatic evening clothes, lavished with fur and intricately cut. He definitely does not believe in the "Less is more" dictum. Nor does he feel clothes should be unstructured.

His appeal is wide. In 1975, when he held a retrospective show of his twenty-year work in fashion, Mamie Eisenhower and Sophia Loren both sent the same scooped-neck navy brocade dress to be presented.

"If a woman buys five pieces, that's ten

thousand dollars," he says, when asked if custom-made clothes can turn a profit. "When we started, we charged five hundred dollars for a day dress. Today we can't put one out for less than twelve hundred," he explains. But he's happy to point out that some prices for ready-to-wear clothes are just as high.

Many of his customers are women who are used to having their clothes made to order. Some bring their daughters for a special dress —a debutante gown or a wedding dress—and that brings a new generation of clients.

The designer was born Arnold Isaacs in Montreal, studied dressmaking in Paris and worked for Paquin, a French couturier, before coming to New York in 1951 to work with Charles James. During a time when he was doing free-lance work, a photographer decided his credit would read "Scaasi." The name was, of course, Isaacs spelled backwards, and somehow it caught on. When a headwaiter greeted him as "Mr. Scaasi," he accepted the new name.

Making custom clothes is what he has always wanted to do. "I'm happy with my life," he says. "There are enough women in this country who appreciate good clothes. They may not buy everything from me, but when they want something special they come in."

197

Adele Simpson

"Traditional" is the word for Adele Simpson. Her family life is traditional. So are her clothes.

"Going into a fitting room with a woman is very revealing," she says. "Give her a new color, a new fabric and a new silhouette all at the same time and she can't absorb it. She becomes confused. Very often, she walks out of the store with a new dress that looks very much like the one she wore when she came in. She worries about what her husband will think, what her children will think.

"I've been to cities where the women will ask me, 'Has the dress been advertised?' What they're worrying about is that other people will know what they pay for their clothes.

"Designers are often carried away. They make sensational things. I'm tempted that way myself. But you have to remember if you are in business that your clothes have to pay off. I have a lot of people employed. I worry about keeping our factories busy. Before I make anything, I have to think: Will women buy it? Will it be profitable? Women are very smart. They know what they need to fit into their lives. It's lovely to look up at the sky and think about making a sky-blue chiffon dress, but if nobody wants it, it's foolish to spend your time on it."

Adele Simpson's dresses are security blankets for scores of women around the country who know she will never embarrass them by putting her label on a dress that is bizarre. Her clothes are known as sure sellers—on the fashion beat, but never ahead of it.

Still, even Mrs. Simpson is sometimes astounded at how cautious women can be. "I remember trying to sell Pat Nixon a pants suit when she was in the White House. She wore pants that she picked up in some sports store in California and I thought she should have some that were made for her. I showed her a white jacket with navy pants and she asked me if it was wash-and-wear—she was afraid she couldn't get good dry cleaning done."

Adele Simpson was born Adele Smithline,

the youngest of a family of five girls, all of whom took embroidery lessons so when they got married they could embroider their own towels and linen. She studied dressmaking at Pratt Institute and made dresses for her sister, Anne, who worked for Ben Gershel, a coat and suit house.

"Who makes your clothes?" her employer asked Anne.

"My kid sister," she answered. He promptly gave the kid sister a job.

"The first dress I made there was a pleated skirt and a middy blouse," she recalled. "I did away with all the complicated underpinnings they were making then. It was a very simple style."

Anne left to marry Cyril Magnin, the West Coast retailer, but Adele stayed on to have one of the more enduring designing careers on Seventh Avenue.

The minute she married Wesley Simpson, a textile producer, she changed her professional name. (They were married for forty-four years until his death in 1976.) Soon there were two children, Jeffrey and Joan, who grew up in Greenwich, Connecticut. When Jeffrey was fifteen and Joan ten, Mrs. Simpson took the summer off to get to know them and to decide whether she wanted to take over Mary Lee, the company for which she then worked. When she decided to try it, her husband bought a town house off Fifth Avenue and the family moved to the city.

"We made a pact—no business talk at the dinner table," she recalls. "But as the children grew up that's all they wanted to talk about. It was hard to get them to stop." Both children are now in the dress business. Joan and her husband, Richard Raines, work with Mrs. Simpson. Jeff has his own company, Casi.

Recently Mrs. Simpson gave her collection of a hundred and fifty costumes she picked up in countries such as Turkey, India, China and Japan to the Fashion Institute of Technology, to be used by the students. Along with them went fifteen hundred books on fabrics, costumes and paintings that she had collected. There were also dolls and dolls' clothes and photographs that her husband, an amateur photographer, made on their travels. "I used to use these things in my work," she says. "An embroidery pattern would give me an idea for a print. A uniform would give me a detail for a coat. In some cases I could match up a dress I made with the costume that contributed to it."

She is now the grandmother of three, all boys. Jeffrey and his wife, Stephanie, have one son; Joan and Richard have two. She's proud of her grandsons, but a little wistful. "It's a pity there's no girl," she says. She means someone she could make dresses for, and hand on the business to in the third generation.

Charles Suppon

Charles Suppon is a young man in a hurry. "I like to do things fast," he says. When his showroom was being redecorated, he insisted that a shower, kitchen and dining room be installed "so when I'm working, I don't have to go home—I can stay right here and work straight through." He moved into a hotel "so someone else can do the cleaning and the housekeeping."

Things have happened to him quickly. Be-

fore his first year in Intre-Sport, his own business, was over, he was nominated for a Coty Award. He's designing the kind of adventuresome sports clothes he likes to make ("Thank God, they don't come to us for classic Shetland sweaters in four different colors") and he's making money at it. Stores like Saks Fifth Avenue and Bonwit Teller are competing with each other to be the first to open Suppon shops.

To everyone, he's the hot new designer, the one to watch.

His clothes are sold in major stores all over the country. In addition to his women's sportswear, he has introduced a line of men's

202

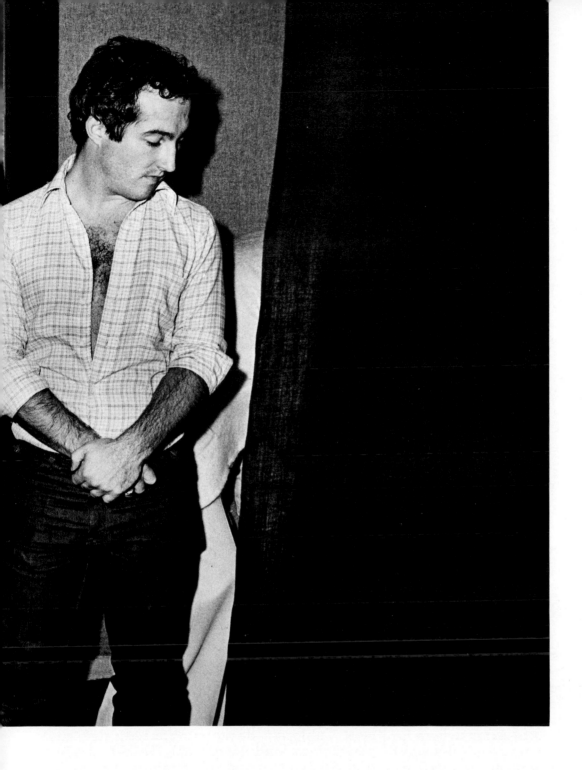

clothes, which have also found a following. He's thinking about expanding his sphere still further. "I want to do serious swimsuits and next year I'd like to add evening clothes, maybe suede with lace or chamois with lace—it would be interesting, coming from a sportswear background, to go into more formal things."

Suppon missed the agony and travail many young designers undergo before they get their chance. Right after graduating from school in Chicago—he was born in Collinsville, Illinois, a small town near St. Louis—he went to work as Calvin Klein's assistant. For six years he learned everything he could about fashion, including the business angle. When the chance came to start his own company, he was ready.

Still, he doesn't know how long he'll hang around in the fashion industry. "I give myself until I'm thirty-five," he says. "Maybe by then I will have said everything I have to say. I don't want to just turn out clothes. I want them to look fresh, to be exciting."

What will he do in seven years?

He has the answer to that too. "The theater," he says quickly. "I love the theatrical side of the fashion business—the shows, working with models, that sort of thing. That may be where I'll end up."

Gustave Tassell

For most of his life, Gustave Tassell was a man pursued by a demon. The demon was Norman Norell, for a long time considered the dean of American designers. It was not altogether a bad thing for Tassell.

He was born in Philadelphia and, after an obligatory stint in the U.S. Army, where he was trained as a dental surgeon's assistant "because I was good with my hands," he moved to a Greenwich Village cold-water flat to live the Bohemian life and learn to paint. To support himself, he got a job in the advertising and display department at Hattie Carnegie. A towering figure in the fashion world, she operated a specialty store that carried custom-made clothes as well as ready-to-wear. Examining the Norell styles there, Mr. Tassell decided he would be a designer. He bought a figure at a dressmaker's supply store and taught himself how to cut, sew and drape.

After a few jobs he left for Europe, where he supported himself by selling sketches to visiting American buyers for five dollars each. "That is how I met Galanos—he bought four sketches because he felt sorry for me and told me to look him up if I ever came to California." After two years in Paris he returned home and headed West to visit his sister. He decided to stay and Galanos helped him get started in business.

The year was 1956, and clothes, by contemporary standards, were elaborate. The ones Tassell turned out were elegant but simple. They were compared more with Norell's style than with his friend Galanos'. While most California designers concentrated on playclothes and swimsuits, Tassell made pared-down, sophisticated things that were comparable to the clothes in Paris. For sixteen years he and James Galanos kept the high-fashion flag flying in California.

Then, in 1972, Norell died and Gustave Tassell was asked to come East and help the house carry on. For the next four years the credits read: "Norman Norell by Tassell."

"It was a great experience, taking over the workrooms and being exposed to his records. I learned so much," Tassell says. He added his own refinements to the established Norell style until the bubble burst and the executors decided to close the house. But Tassell is equipped to carry on the fine dressmaking tradition in America on his own.

Pauline Trigère

If she hadn't become a fashion designer, she would have liked to be a surgeon, Pauline Trigère insists. "I would have made beautiful incisions and sewn them up magnificently," she says. Or perhaps she would have been an architect, tearing down walls and reconstructing buildings.

But designing was her fate. Her parents were both tailors, arriving in Paris from Odessa in 1905. Her father had made military uniforms in his native Russia. In Paris he served as a contractor for such department stores as Galeries Lafayette and Bon Marché. Her mother had a boutique. The workrooms were in the back of the apartment in which she grew up in Paris.

"I learned the trade by watching others. Sometimes my father gave me some money to help out and I studied how people worked. I had no real training. I went to school, because one goes to school when one is young, but there was no one to advise me. My parents were too busy making a living to concern themselves with such things."

So Pauline was married early—to Lazar Radley, a coat and suit manufacturer. Her father died in 1932, and five years later she set out to build a new life in Chile, with her mother, her brother Robert, her husband and two young sons, Jean-Pierre and Philippe. The specter of Hitler was hanging over Europe and it seemed wise to get out.

The family stopped off in New York to visit relatives, and Adele Simpson, whom Pauline had met in Europe, urged her to stay in this country. She got her a job at Ben Gershel, where she was working, and later as an assistant to Travis Banton at Hattie Carnegie. She was fired the week before Christmas, soon after Pearl Harbor.

The next month she and her brother went into business with $1,500 in borrowed money. A diamond brooch brought an additional $800 when it was pawned. In some ways it was an auspicious time to start a fashion business. The war was to cut off American stores from their design sources in Paris. While the American ready-to-wear industry

Diane Von Furstenberg

Diane Von Furstenberg is the quintessential modern woman. Married and divorced. On good terms with her husband. Mother of two children—a girl and a boy. To some women she is not just a dress designer, she is a role model. Beautiful and self-assured, she is willing to play the part. In many ways she identifies with these women. That, in part, explains why they do not resent her, why they take her advice on what to wear—and a lot of other things.

"Be easy about your clothes. Forget about them," she says in her *Book of Beauty*, published in 1976. It's subtitled "How to become a more attractive, confident and sensual woman," and it pretty much draws upon her life experience.

"Don't go against your own nature," she writes. "Don't go against yourself. If you are short, don't wear very high heels. What is important is to find a style for yourself. Find clothes that are appealing and attractive and that you feel good in. Stick with them."

She is enthusiastic about being a woman. "I am more sure of myself than I have ever been," she says. "I know what I am, and what women can do. I know what women want. There's been a big change in women in the last few years. It's not a question of age or background. It's a question of being a woman in today's society. You don't sit around in little white gloves and big hats and try to look fashionable. You have a job, a husband or a lover, and children. Being liberated doesn't mean being ugly, looking

213

like a truckdriver. It means being free to do what you want to do, to be productive, to be honest.''

She did not always feel like this. Born Diane Halfin, in Belgium, of a middle-class Jewish family, she went to boarding schools from the time her parents separated when she was thirteen. In Geneva, at the age of eighteen, she met Prince Egon Von Furstenberg. ''From the minute I knew I was to become Egon's wife, I decided to have a career,'' she recalls. ''I wanted to find my own identity. I had to.''

For a while, there wasn't a party the Von Furstenbergs didn't attend. They were the bright young jet-set couple of the year, attractive and titled (titles always have a fascination for Americans, despite their denials).

But at the same time Diane was planning a business. She arranged to have some dresses made in Italy. During her pregnancy, she lugged sample cases around to show store buyers. Of course, it didn't hurt to announce that she was ''Princess Von Furstenberg.'' It won her entry, but it was the dresses that sold her. They were simple jersey affairs that fit the needs of women who wanted to wear a dress, not jeans. They worked on slim women as well as full ones. Her success was an overnight affair: ''There was a need for my things,

for very simple dresses everyone could wear. A girl who graduates from law school—she can't wear the same jeans she wore in college. A secretary who has to dress suitably at work. These are the women who bought my dresses, along with senators' wives and businessmen's wives.

"Egon used to bring me other people's designs—a white dress by Madame Grès, a Valentino suit. I used to wear them, but now I have enough confidence to wear my own things. My designs have improved. Now I know what I'm doing. I know what is needed."

When she separated from her husband, Diane Von Furstenberg had enough confidence to drop the "Princess" in front of her name. She had progressed enough to go it alone.

She doesn't go to too many parties these days—just the ones she wants to. She spends every weekend she can in her house in the country, with her children, Alexander, who was born in 1970, and Tatiana, one year younger. Besides dresses, she has a solid cosmetics business and a fine jewelry business. She also designs accessories, furs, shoes, "everything for a woman." Her business is flourishing. Diane Von Furstenberg started as a glamour girl. She's turned into a liberated woman.

Chester Weinberg

Designers were coming of age in America during the 1960's. They were coming out of the back rooms, where they had been hidden for years. They became known as Geoffrey (Beene), Bill (Blass), Oscar (de la Renta), Jacques (Tiffeau) and Donald (Brooks) to the "in" crowd. They were invited to fashionable dinner parties. They decorated charity balls. Society women came to their openings.

And suddenly, as the decade was half over, there was a sixth entrant in the charmed circle, Chester. Chester Weinberg. A poor boy from Brooklyn, who knew nothing of the world of fashion until he went to the High School of Music and Art as a small, wispy boy not yet in his teens. "That's when I saw my first Claire McCardell dress, copper jewelry, Capezio shoes," he recalls. "It was mind-blowing. It was art I was interested in then. When I had this exposure, I realized for the first time that instead of being the head of the art department in a local high school, I could become a fashion designer."

The poor boy from Brooklyn caught on quickly. At the Parsons School of Design, he decided to make a gray-flannel dinner suit. He had to go to Orchard Street, on the Lower East Side, to find the material—it didn't exist in women's fabric stores at the time. Norman Norell liked it and gave him some white silk satin to work with.

Ann Keagy, his teacher and today the head of the school's fashion department, remembers him as a brilliant student. She still calls him "my baby." He was sixteen when he entered Parsons. He graduated first in his class.

Then came the apprenticeship in Seventh Avenue's back rooms, striving always to get into higher-priced houses so he could work with better fabrics, try more inventive designs. There were high spots: "I went to Europe, I saw Balenciaga, I was invited to Jacques Fath's parties, I danced with Ginger Rogers at Schiaparelli." And there were low points too: "I was discouraged because American designers, including me, were copying Europe. I wanted the American thing to begin to happen."

When Geoffrey Beene got star billing at Teal Traina, he felt it was beginning to happen. "I followed his career with admiration," he recalls. "I identified with him. When I heard he was leaving to start his own firm, I wondered who would get his job. It was a plum job." It turned out that Chester Weinberg got the job. But he never got his name on the label. Manufacturers were still leery of giving a designer too much exposure for fear they would do exactly what Geoffrey Beene did: start his own business.

After three years it was Chester Weinberg's turn. And so, in 1966, there was that first collection with "Chester Weinberg" on the door and on the label. And the society women in the chairs and the fitting rooms: Judy Peabody, Baby Jane Holzer, Amanda Burden, Isabel Eberstadt, Sisi Kahan—all the beautiful people. Just one collection and he was catapulted into the rarefied circle of big names in American fashion. It was an exceptional collection. At a time when tough chic was in, he made pretty dresses. Instead of hard-edged tailoring, he used ruffles. Suit jackets were shapely. For evening, there were long organdy dresses. "It was really opposing Courrèges," he said. "I didn't think clothes should be so severe. I thought women ought to look pretty."

But he didn't stay with pretty dresses. He went on evolving his style. He turned to matte jersey. He pared down his designs, always simplifying. He put a peace button on his bridal dress. He moved into skinny sweater dresses, turtleneck dresses. But in the debacle that followed the introduction of the midi in 1970, his company folded. Undercapitalized, it couldn't survive until fashion got back into favor. Today Chester Weinberg designs cashmere sweaters for Ballantyne, dresses for Jones New York, ready-to-wear for Hanro. He has joined the growing army of free-lance designers, which is one of the big developments of the 1970's. He has his name on the labels.

I introduced myself to Bernadine Morris over the phone about a year and a half ago, and even before we had made a date to look at my photographs, she told me she would like to work on *The Fashion Makers* with me. I consider her to be one of the most important fashion writers in the world, and it was a great privilege to have her collaboration in this project.

A very special thank you to Kevin Walz, my husband, for his encouragement from the moment this project was first conceived. He spent many hours with me working on the proposal, examining contact sheets, editing photographs, bearing with my craziness and designing this book beautifully.

My guiding light at Random House was my editor, Gail Winston. During all the ups and downs a book must go through, Gail believed and promoted and is directly responsible for the wonderful way in which this book was handled. My gratitude to Michele Koury, Bernie Klein, Sono Rosenberg and Bob Scudellari who played an important part in the production.

My friend Joan Grady gave me my first job photographing a designer. It was wonderful to have a friend who had confidence in me

Acknowledgments

when I began my career. Neil Bieff and Arturo Herréra, two very special designers, were my first regular clients and became most cherished friends. Vicky Wilson saw the possibility for this book when she looked at my portfolio during an interview and really set the project in motion for me.

My agent, Wendy Weil, sold Random House on the idea of introducing the faces of fashion to America. Wendy, with her assistant Martha Levin, put the initial excitement into the concept and saw that Random House was the publisher where we belonged.

Jill Krementz has affected my life since the first time I heard her speak at New York University. We later became friends, and without her I never would have figured out how to be reasonably organized.

The many people who listened to me and who gave opinions, ideas and all sorts of boosting and encouragement were Ron Lieberman, Susan McCaslin, Anla Cheng, Stanley and Ellen Fellerman, Pucci Meyer, Chris Steinmetz and Tammy Hendershot. Ellen Stern, Ira Shapiro, Joan Oliver, Michele Stephenson, Michael Longacre and Stanley Stellar were editors who gave the book its first published publicity, so long ago. I am most thankful to my friends at *The New York Times*, especially Carrie Donovan for my most enjoyable assignments and Ruth Ansel for her art direction on them.

My invaluable assistant, Bonnie West, worked with me in the developing, printing and editing of all my pictures. She helped me get through deadlines and traumas and I am most grateful for her help. Very special thank yous to my friend Peter Perin, Drs. Edward Beattie and Ralph Marcove and my parents, Pauline and Stanley Turner.

Lastly, I am most grateful to Bill Blass for eating my apples and tossing one in the air—thus creating my favorite photograph. He patiently spent much time with me while I was working on this project. And to John Anthony, who first introduced me to Bernadine and gave me direction when I needed it. These two, and the other fashion makers in this book, were my inspiration. I send my love and appreciation to them and their friends, co-workers, models and the many others whom I met in the fashion industry.

B.W.

223

BARBRA WALZ studied photography at Pratt Institute and is a free-lance photographer living in New York City. She has traveled throughout the United States and Europe photographing people in their environments. Her photographs have been exhibited both here and abroad. Her work has appeared in the *New York Times, Vogue, The Village Voice, People, New York Magazine* and other publications.

BERNADINE MORRIS was born in New York City. A graduate of Hunter College, with a master's degree in English literature from New York University, in 1963 she joined *The New York Times,* where she specializes in fashion reporting. A co-author of *American Fashion,* she was also fashion feature editor of *Women's Wear Daily.* She is the mother of two teenage children and lives with her family in New York City.